Oscar Pistorius was born in 1986 in Johannesburg, South Africa. Known as the 'Blade Runner' and 'the fastest man on no legs', Pistorius is the double-amputee world-record holder in the 100m, 200m and 400m events, and runs with the aid of Cheetah Flex-Foot carbon fibre transtibial artificial limbs.

BLADE RUNNER

Oscar Pistorius was born with no fibulae. His parents' decision to have both his legs amputated was to give him the best chance of a normal life. His mother wrote him a letter: 'A loser is not one who runs last in the race. It is the one who sits and watches, and has never tried to run.' Running on prosthetic legs, he's now a world-renowned athlete, winning three gold medals at the 2008 Beijing Paralympics, breaking a Paralympic record for the 200m and a world record for the 400m. His ultimate fight now is to compete at the 2012 Olympics.

OSCAR PISTORIUS

BLADE RUNNER

Complete and Unabridged

ULVERSCROFT
Leicester

First published in Great Britain in 2009 by
Virgin
The Random House Group Limited
London

First Large Print Edition
published 2010
by arrangement with
The Random House Group Limited
London

British Library CIP Data

Pistorius, Oscar, *1986 –*
Blade runner.
1. Pistorius, Oscar, *1986 –* 2. Runners (Sports)- -
South Africa- -Biography. 3. Amputees- -South Africa- -
Biography. 4. Large type books.
I. Title II. Pistorius, Oscar, *1986 –* Dream runner.
796.4′22′092–dc22

ISBN 978–1–44480–100–2

Published by
F. A. Thorpe (Publishing)
Anstey, Leicestershire

Set by Words & Graphics Ltd.
Anstey, Leicestershire
Printed and bound in Great Britain by
T. J. International Ltd., Padstow, Cornwall

This book is printed on acid-free paper

Contents

Introduction

'The real loser is never the person who crosses the finishing line last. The real loser is the person who sits on the side, the person who does not even try to compete.' My mother wrote these words to me in a letter when I was still a small baby, about five months before my surgeons performed my bilateral amputation. She kept the letter for me to read as an adult.

I have always wanted to participate and compete. I wanted to run, to swim, to play cricket and rugby, to drive a car and, of course, a motorbike. I have always wanted to live life normally. To tell you the truth, I don't think of myself as disabled. I have limits, but we all have limits and like anyone else I also have many talents.

This attitude is integral to how my family approaches life and their philosophy has made me the man I am today: 'This is Oscar Pistorius, exactly as he should be. Perfect in himself.'

My brother, my sister and I were brought

up with one iron rule — no one was allowed to say: 'I can't.'

Perhaps this is what has made my life so special. Over the years I have had the opportunity to speak with many people (and I have also read their letters and messages to me), and I have come to understand how my example can be an inspiration to those who, like me, have experienced and struggled with a physical problem, but who don't want to give up and settle for second best. This can also be true for others who have had to overcome obstacles of a different nature in their lives.

It is for this reason that I have decided to tell my story: the story of a young boy surrounded by love, support and the courage of his family; of a young man who experienced the most profound grief with the loss of his adored mother and of a man who is chasing his dream — a dream to become an athlete. Not a disabled athlete, simply an athlete.

Oscar

BLADE RUNNER

1

Fingerprints

My name is Oscar Carl Lennard Pistorius. I was born to Sheila and Henk Pistorius on 22 November 1986 at the Sandton Clinic in Johannesburg. According to my parents I was a beautiful baby, weighing in at a healthy 3 kilos and 300 grams, but unbeknownst to them, I had been born with an important bone missing in each leg: the fibula. Along with the tibia, this bone extends from the ankle to the knee and supports the full weight of the body. In addition my feet were malformed: they were lacking in the outer part. Simply put, each foot had only two toes — the big toe and the index — the inner bones and the heel. None of the medical staff present at my birth noted the malformation of my little feet; it was my father who first noticed their difference, and so it was that my parents began asking the first in a long series of questions. It was clear in their minds that they would do whatever it was going to take to find a solution.

Fortunately for me, I have never needed to press those around me for answers: right from the start everything was out in the open, and countless times I have heard the story of the trips my parents made to various medical luminaries to ask their advice in the months following my birth. My parents have never been shy or embarrassed to discuss my situation, both with me and in front of me, as well as my siblings, or for that matter with the many friends and acquaintances who made their way to our house for different reasons and inevitably asked for updates on my medical situation. My parents took the time to answer the questions clearly and simply, explaining what they knew, why they had set out on a pilgrimage of sorts to consult the best doctors in the field and why they sought second or third (often totally different) opinions on my case. Each step along the road gave them greater knowledge, both of the physical problem and what my options would be. No one was able to discourage them. I have a profound respect for them because it cannot have been easy, but then again the Pistoriuses are a stubborn people.

The confusion must have been particularly difficult for my parents because my situation was not straightforward: my condition was both complicated and rare. With the malformation of my lower legs at birth, the fact that I would never walk and that I would be wheelchair-reliant seemed to many a foregone conclusion. My parents saw things differently, and so they began to research all the alternatives that would allow me to lead the most 'normal' life possible. By the time they came to a decision they had met with eleven amputation specialists and worked their way through a barrage of ideas.

At the end of every consultation, my father would ask the surgeon one question: 'If it was your child, and you were unable to operate yourself, who would you turn to?' In this way, my parents were able to tap into a network of extraordinary surgeons and trusted hands; although this was not absolute protection from charlatans, it was more effective than you might initially expect.

Over time my father developed quite an expertise on the subject: he had read and researched the condition extensively and listened attentively to the explanations given by the various experts, so that when he found himself in front of a surgeon who recommended what was in his opinion too drastic an amputation (i.e. above the knee as opposed to below the knee, which made no sense given that the joint was perfectly fine) he steadfastly refused to pay the bill. This is an excellent example of the Pistorius attitude to life; my father could not forgive the doctor the flippancy with which he had given his advice. In his view it was professionally irresponsible. The surgeon must have understood the error of his ways because when my father replied to his bill with a bill of his own itemising his own expenses, we never heard from him again.

Throughout that consultation period my parents kept an archive, which contains all the medical opinions and documents relating to my condition. They were totally preoccupied by what and who I would become and also how, as an adult, I would feel about their decision. They wanted to make sure that if, when I looked back and reflected on their choices, I was unhappy with the turns my life had taken, I would be able to go back and understand the rationale behind their decision. They had to take decisions on my behalf, but the wide-ranging views of the various doctors they had consulted made them doubly conscious of the gravity of their choice. I can only imagine how hard that decision must have been for them, and how heavily the enormity of that responsibility must have weighed.

Certain doctors proposed to amputate the right foot only and attempt reconstructive surgery on the left, as it was slightly less malformed. After a worldwide search my parents decided to approach the three doctors whom they had found to be the best and ask them to join forces and discuss my case. As luck would have it, one of these three doctors, Gerry Versveld, was South African. Should my parents decide to go ahead and agree to the procedure he would be the surgeon chosen to perform the operation.

Gerry was convinced that if my parents were prepared to make a bold and courageous decision and amputate both my legs below the knee while I was still sufficiently young, I would learn to walk with prostheses and would encounter fewer problems. Basically, if the double amputation was performed before I learnt to walk, I would never know what it was like to walk on my own feet and so would not suffer from the trauma of having lost them. Gerry also told my parents that he had already successfully performed this type of operation and that the results were very good. In addition, he had presented my case for discussion at an important American international amputation congress in which the top specialists worldwide were participating, in order to garner further information and generate more opinions on the case: he had encountered unanimous support for the option of a bilateral amputation.

What proved decisive for my parents was when they asked to meet a couple of young children who had already undergone the operation, in order to see how they walked and to gain an idea of what they could expect for my future. They were amazed as they arrived at the Prosthetics Centre in Pretoria when they realised that the young man they had been watching run around the garden a few minutes earlier was the same young man who was waiting to meet them. They had never imagined that anyone who had undergone a bilateral amputation could be so agile and were terribly impressed by the young man's quiet confidence as he calmly told them his story.

Mirroring what certain doctors had suggested in my case, this boy, who was twelve at the time of the meeting, had undergone various reconstructive surgeries as a baby. Somehow, and with considerable effort on his part, he had learnt to walk, but it was not easy, and he moved with such awkwardness and lack of coordination that his first two years at school were nightmarish as the children continually mocked him. The youngsters teased and excluded him from their games because he was different and they assumed his lopsided gait meant that he was mentally deficient. He was a lonely and sad child. Then his parents met Gerry Versveld, and together they decided to abandon the project of reconstructive surgery and moved to amputate both legs. After the operation, and with prostheses, he learnt to walk easily and even play sport. His family decided to change schools and give him a fresh start as an 'ordinary child', and he was now very happy and felt he and his parents had made the right decision.

Meeting this young man made all the difference for my parents. There before them was an adolescent who was happy, healthy, sporty and independent, a perfect example of what my parents hoped I could become in the future. His opportunities and freedoms were exactly what they dreamed of for me.

And so, months after that initial round-table discussion, the decision was taken to undergo the amputation. When I was eleven months old Dr Gerry Versveld went ahead and operated. He is a wonderful human being and a true gentleman; over the last twenty years he has become a dear friend to both my family and me. We have a very special relationship: Gerry has played a vital role in my life, both as a physician and as a friend, and I was simply delighted when he travelled to support me during the Paralympics in Athens in 2004.

One of my father's favourite stories from this period in our lives concerns the day of my operation. He was out of town on business and in the midst of an important meeting when the tension proved too much. He stood up, excused himself, and explained that he needed to leave as his son was undergoing a bilateral amputation. He took the next available flight but only arrived at the hospital that evening, long after the operation was over. As he stepped into the ward he heard me wailing in agony. He asked the nurses if I had been given enough or the correct dose of pain-relief medication, and as none of the nurses seemed capable of answering his question, with typical Pistorius grit he managed to get his hands on my medical folder. He discovered to his horror that as the nurses had been unable to find the correct pain-relief medication they had given me a much milder analgesic. He immediately phoned Gerry, who rushed to the hospital still in his pyjamas and kicked up a storm; from then on I was treated like a little prince.

Just over six months later, at only seventeen

months old, I received my first pair of prosthetic legs. Constructed of plaster and mesh, with a lycra 'skin' that was even flesh-coloured, they were made to measure for me and surprisingly comfortable. I loved them; from that day onwards I became invincible, a wild child. It became my raison d'être to find the highest and most unlikely places to climb, succeed and then start all over again. My energy was boundless, and I saw no reason why my new legs would not be able to take me everywhere I needed or wanted to go.

I believe that it was at this time in my life that my personality was shaped, and that my family was instrumental in laying the foundation stones of my competitive nature and of the man that I am today. Carl, my brother, was eighteen months old when I was born, and it was clear from the start that I would follow him wherever he led me, and certainly into any mischievous adventure. He would push me to my limit and then beyond; we were just like Buzz and Woody in *Toy Story*.

Wherever Carl went, I was by his side, and our parents, instead of stopping me or slowing us down — after all, I was a child that people labelled 'disabled' — pushed me forward, encouraging me to try everything, especially every type of physical activity. With hindsight, I have begun to appreciate just how difficult it must have been for them to give me all that freedom, fighting their natural instincts to shield me from potential harm. In allowing me that freedom my parents taught me to be independent, to defend myself and to take care of myself whatever the circumstances, however daunting the challenge.

By the age of two I was a real menace, with blond shoulder-length curls and a short fringe (I am still mortified today when I see pictures of myself and the mullet); it was around this time that I received my first pair of legs with the wooden foot part covered in rubber. In the eighties Nike had not yet started producing Nike Total 90s for babies, but I loved my little shoes with Mickey Mouse emblazoned on their toes. They were extremely cool and allowed me to start putting distance between the more traditional trainers — known in South Africa as 'takkies' — and myself.

At around three years of age I began fully to understand that my feet were different. I had no interest in whether they were better or worse than other feet, just that they were different. Every morning while Carl put on his shoes, I would slip on my prostheses; it was all the same to me. I had two pairs of shoes: my Mickey Mouse pair was for everyday use and another smarter version for my Sunday best and parties. If for some reason I missed church on Sunday I could wear the same pair of shoes for two weeks solid. I realise that it may strike the reader as odd, but the thought that I could wear the same shoes for a hundred days in a row and they would still smell new tickles me silly even now. I consider it one of the advantages of not having any feet.

In February 1989, Aimée our sister was born. My mother used to tell me that during her pregnancy Carl and I never left her side, always wanting to stroke her tummy. We would squabble endlessly, saying, 'She is my sister!', 'No, she is MY sister!' From birth I was spellbound by her feet and kept kissing them. As a small child I was unable to pronounce her name and so I called her 'Gugu'. She would be asleep in her cradle and I would bound up, welcoming her with a 'Helloo Gugu' or by humming her a tune. Inevitably I would wake her, which would then set her off crying, so my parents took to hiding her in places I could not disturb her. I don't remember much more from those days — I was too little — but clearly we have always been a tight-knit family.

Then came the dogs. Each of us had one and, what's more, we had been allowed the dog of our choice. Carl chose a Doberman, Aimée a basset-hound and I selected an American pit-bull called Vivian who, despite the stereotype, was not at all aggressive. If the truth were told Vivian was entirely useless and rather dim and she just slept all day long. Vivian also snored, very loudly. Once my father recorded her while she was sleeping and then went to my mother and played it to her, tricking her into thinking she was listening to herself. Our mother fell for the ploy hook, line and sinker. She was so embarrassed that she went out and acquired the latest 'cure all' medicines. The entire family played along and I don't think we ever told her that it was a joke. What my father never knew was that my mother had bought the incredibly expensive magical anti-snore cushion on his credit card (it cost well over £400 in today's currency). Unfortunately, after a while, Vivian's personality changed and we caught her attacking one of the tortoises we had in the garden. My dad became increasingly concerned that Vivian might do us children some harm, and eventually took her to a veterinary practice. We never saw her again.

Every year, during the December holidays,

my family decamped to our holiday home in Plettenberg Bay; the car journey was epic in length. My recollections of those interminable journeys are bittersweet, because my father, in true hard-headed family style, made it a question of pride to complete the entire 1,200 kilometres in one stretch. To make matters worse I suffered terribly from carsickness, and so the kilometres passed in a queasy blur. One can be sure that the lunch boxes or padkos that my father prepared for each of us — which contained delicacies like banana milk and fish paste rolls, his favourite foods — did little to ease my nausea.

About 300 kilometres before Plettenberg Bay the monotony of the trip lifted somewhat; this was where my father took his short cut. It was really just a single dust road that passed between two rather steep hills but, being about 80 kilometres long, it doubled wonderfully as our annual rally track.

By the time the rally was over we knew that we were about to see the ocean. The first person that spotted it won the largest remaining slab of chocolate. Aimée was still very little when she became our reigning champion spotter. In truth, Aimée would shout 'I see the ocean!' at every corner, and even though Carl and I protested that there was nothing yet to see, our father would proclaim her the champion and hand over the chocolate. Whether this was due to her hawk-like eyesight or simply because she was always well behaved and obedient was open to question — what is certain, however, is that she was the apple of her daddy's eye.

The rest of the family were encouraged to take a particular attitude to Aimée. Our father always instructed us to treat her like a 'lady'. When we were all in the car together we had to open the door for her; she would sit up front with Dad and we boys would sit in the back. She was spoilt rotten. Whenever we argued our father would immediately ask us, 'Did you treat her like a lady?' and we boys (with the logic peculiar to seven-or eight-year-old children) were easily taken with the allure of behaving like 'gentlemen'. There were inevitable lapses. On one occasion I remember pushing Aimée; she went straight to our father in tears, but I justified my actions by explaining that her behaviour had not been at all ladylike.

I remember vividly one holiday in Plettenberg Bay. I was racing up and down the beach when two slightly older children approached me. When they asked why my feet only left holes in the sand instead of footprints I simply explained that those holes were my footprints! 'Ahh . . . ' they exclaimed, and then began running behind me on their heels trying to leave the same type of footprint. I have never forgotten that day. Although I did not yet have the maturity to grasp the concept in such clear terms, it was the day on which I understood that people see you exactly as you see yourself, and I was relaxed and confident.

As well as our annual trip to the bay, we were in the habit of going away at weekends. We particularly liked going hiking for two or three days, sometimes walking up to 20 kilometres a day, and on these occasions the same rules were applicable to each of us. We each carried a rucksack on our back and were allowed to choose both the type and quantity of food and drink for our bag, on the understanding that my parents, who were very strict about us carrying whatever we brought, would oblige us to sit down and eat if the bag became too heavy. The only person they fussed over was Aimée, making sure that she could keep up with us and did not tire. I was never a concern: if anything their difficulty with me was quite the opposite, since I loved hiking and would often set off ahead, leaving them behind, then drop my rucksack at our next appointed resting spot and run back to meet them. I loved running.

Among the happiest recollections of those

idyllic holidays — memories which have remained with me ever since — were the special moments we shared in the car. I was always delighted when my father raced his car: I was born with a fully developed passion for both cars and motorbikes. I can't say for sure, naturally, but it wouldn't surprise me if my first word was 'car' . . .

When I was about three years old my mother drove a red Ford Laser. I thought that it was the coolest car on four wheels. Even at that age I crowed with pride and boasted to all and sundry. My mother's best friend, Gill, clearly remembers me telling people that my mother drove what I called a 'ford lather — WOW!'

But it was my father who really inspired my love of cars. When I was a boy he drove a dark-red two-door Mercedes sports car with leather interior. I just adored driving around with him with the sunroof open. As soon as he stopped at the traffic lights I would jump on the seats in my best effort to stick my head out through the sunroof and imitate, at least as far as I was concerned, film stars touring Hollywood in their limousines. This was the highlight of my week. My father travelled a lot on business so it was also a special occasion to spend some time with him.

When I was four, Dad bought Carl and me

a little blue 60cc off-road vehicle. There was no holding us back. Any downhill incline was fair game, the steeper the better. I was in love; I am certain that had it been possible I would have parked it next to my bed each evening and slept alongside it. Over the next three years Carl and I became little adrenalin junkies, haring around in our beloved car.

Then came a serious and sudden blow. I was seven years old when my parents announced they were getting divorced and we had to sell our home. We stayed with our mother and moved into a smaller house nearer town and so our freewheeling adventures had to come to an end. My mother tried to make sure that we had a couple of outings a month where we could have free rein behind our steering wheel, but it was never quite the same.

2

Made to Measure

What set my childhood apart from that of my siblings, and at times made it tiresome for me, was the fact that my legs required constant attention. It seemed that no sooner had I got a new pair of prostheses than something inevitably needed adjusting. I realised I had to make the most of that initial moment when my legs felt like a perfect fit, for it would be only a couple of weeks before I began to grow out of them. The prostheses would begin to hurt my stumps and we would have to restart the procedure all over again.

My parents took this problem very seriously indeed: Gerry Versveld had explained the potential dangers to amputees of using incorrectly sized prosthetics. Blisters and sores can form on the point of contact, and if these worsen further amputation is often necessary. The risk is particularly serious for people who, like me, have undergone a bilateral amputation of the legs because, unlike someone who has lost an arm, we are obliged to place our entire body weight on the prosthetics.

This prudence has remained with me, particularly where my training is concerned; if I develop a blister or bleed as a result of my skin chafing from the friction, I stop training and rest my limbs. This was one of the reasons why Gerry had wanted to amputate as little as possible during the original surgery: that way should I encounter problems of this type, further surgery would still be an option.

The average life span of my prostheses was, at best, a couple of months. Getting a new pair inevitably involved endless waiting as the technicians took my measurements and then adjusted and readjusted them until the fit was perfect. At the time technology was a far cry from today's standards. Prostheses were made from solid plaster and glass fibre with a wooden foot and a rubber sole all attached. They were seriously heavy for a small boy, weighing an astonishing 3 kilograms.

I was about four years old when, for the first time, it dawned on me that artificial legs boasted certain advantages over the real thing. It was also then that I began to grasp the differences between mine and other more old-fashioned legs. On one occasion I was whiling away my afternoon playing my preferred video games while Carl played with his favourite go-kart, which our uncle, his godfather, had built for him over the Christmas holidays. The kart was his pride and joy, and no one was allowed to touch it, let alone take it out for a spin. It was made with a steel frame and aluminium boxes for seats. The wheels had been bolted onto the frame and then connected up by means of a rope attached to the front axle, which made steering possible.

At the time we were living in Johannesburg in a house right on top of a hill; it boasted great views of the city but more importantly a steep, straight road that connected it to the suburbs below. That afternoon I was happily doing my own thing when Carl came into the room. He stood silently, staring at me, before coming up to me and taking my hand to lead me out onto the driveway where his flame-red and blue go-kart was waiting for us. Not in my wildest dreams did I expect to be allowed on board, but to my astonishment Carl invited me to sit down behind him. He took the wheel and with a slight push and a yank on the right-hand rope we began to speed down the hill.

Of course, the go-kart was without brakes. Normally Carl would ride it in 'free fall' for about 50 or 60 metres before pulling up onto the embankment next to the road, thereby slowing himself down to a halt. That day, however, we whizzed past his normal cut-off point. I remember it so clearly; I thought he had decided to challenge the laws of physics. I had often watched him flying down the hill but had never heard the wheels rattle quite so. We kept on going: 100 metres, 150, 200 . . .

We were fast approaching the wall at the bottom of our road, and I must confess that if there was ever a moment when I thought it was all over, this was it. We were about to smash at full speed right into the wall when suddenly Carl grabbed my artificial leg and with one crazy six-year-old sweep of his arm managed to shove my leg between the wheel and the tar, so bringing us to a screeching halt — within 20 metres of the wall. Unfortunately this act of braking wiped Mickey Mouse right off my shoes, but it was an exhilarating way to learn that the prostheses, which were so often a source of pain to me, could also be incredibly useful.

I have had my fill of funny (and odd) experiences, particularly when mixing with children ignorant of artificial legs like mine. On one occasion Carl and I were sitting and playing in the beautiful sandpit that our father had built for us. We loved playing there; we would be completely absorbed by cars, building roads, tunnels, dams and bridges. I loved anything that included water. One day we were outside playing when two other children (my father's secretary's children) came to spend the day with us. We hardly knew them. Without warning one of the kids grabbed a wooden pole that we had left lying around and smacked me really hard across my legs. He had worked out that my legs were different, and we had tried to explain to him exactly what prosthesis was, but he could not quite get his head around the idea. With the force of the blow, my plaster and fibre-glass legs shattered into a hundred little pieces, leaving my little wooden feet to go spinning up into the air.

When he saw what he had done the child burst into hysterical tears. He was traumatised as he was convinced that his blow had severed my foot. My mother heard him crying uncontrollably and came out all ready to reprimand us but when she saw the result of his actions, she was furious.

To begin with I too was pretty cross with the boy but when I realised his consternation was real I began to comfort him. I told him not to worry: he had not hurt me; it was only an artificial leg after all.

Thinking back now, I understand my

mother's reaction: the prostheses were expensive and I broke pair after pair.

My father was different. In the aspects of our lives that he considered important he demanded absolute discipline; for the rest he was content to let us be and allow us to follow our own instincts, trusting us when he should have known better.

On one occasion I ended up in the hospital's intensive care unit. I must have been seven or eight, and my brother and sister and I had decided to bake a cake. Our mother was not at home, so we asked our father — who was busy working — for permission and he blithely agreed. Typical of my dad: he thinks children can do whatever they set their minds to, and he had great faith in the capabilities of his own children. You want to bake a cake? Well, go ahead, try. Nothing worried him.

It may not surprise you to learn that we had no recipe to follow. We were intending to copy whatever we had seen our mother do — a bit of this and a bit of that. Our plan was to cook our cake in a saucepan. Carl, as the eldest, had turned on the stove, and had requested that as his helper I get the flour. I was sitting on the work surface and had no wish to climb down and then up again on the other side. I decided, then, to climb across the glass cover that went over the stove; needless to say, I burnt my stumps badly.

Over the years, and even without my active (and irresponsible) contributions, I had plenty of problems with my stumps. My prostheses gave me both blisters and neurofibromatosis — a disorder of the nervous system which causes benign tumours. My nerve endings were growing, but as they lacked the space for development fibromas would appear. They were terribly painful and caused my stumps to become hypersensitive, making any movement and particularly walking impossible for me. I went through patches where I could not leave the house for three or four months at a stretch, not even to attend school. I would have to stay home and study alone. I missed school terribly.

A couple of years after my parents divorced and our madcap adventures came to a temporary end, my father moved to a freehold in Honeydew, just outside Johannesburg. We were delighted as once again we had more space than we could use at our disposition. There was even a rather dusty football pitch full of weeds and stones. Sometimes Carl and I would play football with the local township kids, running between the goats and chickens that roamed freely. We did not always understand everything they were telling us: at home we spoke English with my mother's family and Afrikaans with my father's family (there are eleven official languages in South Africa), but it made little real difference. Our joint enthusiasm to play football and run after that ball was more than enough to bridge any language barrier. During the breaks in the matches, Carl and I would take our new friends on terrifying bike rides where ramping over bushes and spinning the wheels were part of the experience. The football pitch was off the beaten track. There was little nearby aside from long grass and small tin huts with their outside fireplaces. It was quiet and peaceful. It did not take Carl and me long to realise that it was the ideal place to fly our kites, some of which we had bought and others we had built. At the end of each day spent playing we would head home in our mini Land Rover. If Carl was at the wheel the journey was far quicker, but we inevitably came home covered in scrapes and grazes thanks to his short cuts through the shrubbery. We were unstoppable.

On arriving at the farm you were greeted by a small black gate that was set back from the road and opened onto a dirt track leading up to the house. The track was in fact a long sand road flanked on either side by massive jacaranda trees with their distinctive purple blooms. The little green and white house looked just like a farmhouse. It was the perfect theatre for our adventures.

I loved the place with a fierce intensity. We had all the freedom and the space to express ourselves, be it to drive around in our mini Land Rover, run around or whack golf balls into each corner of the garden.

We spent every second weekend with our dad and often brought friends along. I remember one summer day when, together with my friend Craig, I decided to build the ultimate tree house. I told Craig it had to be the biggest and the best. It was imperative that it have a long tow rope, so that in much the same way as a lift functioned, we would be able to get in and out of the house quickly without having to stop at each of the many floors. I detailed my vision to him as though it was the most straightforward idea in the world. Craig in his turn showed equal naivety and enthusiasm by countering that we needed to find the biggest tree on the property and then choose that tree to be host to our castle.

Quickly we selected an enormous jacaranda tree that was situated between the driveway and the boundary fence. That

29

accomplished, we sat down to write a list of the necessary equipment:

- A hammer (that was sure to reduce our fingers to pulp during the building)
- Nails (that were equally sure to damage our fingers)
- Wooden boards
- A ladder (from which we were certain to tumble)
- A 50-metre steel cable (which, as we quickly learnt, should have been both thicker and more resistant)
- A pulley so we could hang on to something while sliding down the cable
- A rope ladder that we could pull up and hide in the house
- Last, but certainly not least, a sign enforcing our rule: NO GIRLS ALLOWED

It took us two days to collect the necessary provisions (and entailed incursions into builders' yards to obtain the requisite wooden boards). With our very sophisticated architectural plans in hand, fruit of our ten-year-old minds, we began to build the Eighth Wonder of the World. Easy-peasy! The building was straightforward, until we hit our first hitch.

The first floor, a platform of about 2 metres by 1.5 metres, was completed quickly.

We were very proud of ourselves. It was approximately 4 metres from the ground and, although we congratulated one another on its perfection, it was obviously not parallel to the ground. Neither Craig nor I would ever have admitted this though, not even on pain of death. In our opinion, with our first floor finished our building had to keep rising. We started by nailing the planks onto the thickest part of the branch and then built a staircase that led up to the second floor. This floor was designed to be both taller and wider than the first. We were continually traipsing up and down the stairs, collecting more nails, planks and boards and had quite a few close calls, nearly breaking our necks and losing our goods, either by slipping on the stairs or on our lopsided platform. It was a risky business.

By the evening of the third day, we had completed our second floor and, thanks to the experience garnered while building the first one, it was a masterpiece. It was approximately 2.5 metres by 3 metres and was at least 6 metres from the ground (with less than a 5-degree slant). We were very pleased with our building skills and generous with superlatives in our compliments to one another. Craig and I came to the realisation that as adults we would become engineers and go on to build the biggest skyscrapers and bridges that the world had yet to see.

On the morning of the fourth day we concluded that while we grappled with the design of our lift system (basically a rudimentary cable car), the third floor should be delayed. We climbed up onto the second floor and then, with the help of pliers, managed to pull one end of the 50-metre cable right around the tree trunk, as high and as tight as we possibly could, so that it could not slip and cause us to plummet to the ground. Then we let the remainder of the cable fall to the ground. Our plan had been to attach the cable to another tree within 40 metres of our tree house, but I had failed to notice that there weren't any. We had incorrectly measured the distance between our tree house and the chosen arrival and departure point for a cable car by 2 metres. We had not considered that the cable would have to be perfectly taut and that even with the best will in the world and our very strong arms there was simply no way to make it happen. At first we were deflated, but then I hit upon an ingenious solution. All we needed to do was drive my father's old Land Rover over to the foot of the tree, securely attach our steel cable to the tow bar, drive for 40 or so metres until the cable was perfectly taut and then park. As we had decided to build our tree house in a jacaranda that was at the top of a slope, we were convinced that, with the downhill to help us, pulling off our plan would be child's play. We imagined ourselves to be rather like the ancient Egyptians in the process of creating the Pyramids.

From the ground it looked great. Casually Craig said, 'Hey, Oz, I think now is the moment to try out the cable car and see if it works. Why don't you go first?'

Calmly I answered, 'Thanks, my friend, but it is all the same to me. Why don't you go first?'

Silence.

Then we both burst out, at exactly the same time, 'It certainly is high up! Do you think the cable will hold?' Neither of us wanted to be the first to try out the cable: the cable was at least 6.5 metres from the ground and the pulley was showing signs of rust.

Throughout the construction period Aimée, who must have been about eight years old, had been hassling us to let her join in. As we stood pondering our construction, it became clear that there was no real obligation for the tree house to remain an exclusively male domain. In fact, we had come upon the perfect role for Aimée, a position that would allow her to join in the prestigious final phase. She was simply delighted to be included and it never crossed her mind that we were too scared to try out our invention and that this was our only motive for including her. We all returned to the tree, climbed up to the second floor and then instructed Aimée as to what we expected from her. She was to hold tight, very tight, as she was high up.

As Aimée was worried that her grip might become slippery we decided to tie a rope around her wrist and then tie that to the handle. The time had come to take 'one giant leap for mankind' and step out of the jacaranda blossoms, off the platform and towards the Land Rover. At the last moment we decided to tie another piece of rope to the handle, enabling us to control the handle and pull from the ground in order to return the pulley back to the tree house after each descent.

Aimée was ready, or as ready as she was ever going to be, and with a little bit of help (if that's the word) from us, she jumped. We were beside ourselves with excitement; it looked like she was flying!

Unfortunately our grand endeavour was destined to fail. After about 10 metres (and still at least 5 metres above ground) the rusted pulley jammed and Aimée lost her grip on the handlebars: she found herself dangling precariously in mid-air.

Craig and I rolled around laughing while she hollered in despair, regretting ever trusting us. Quickly we climbed down and pulled her to safety. After a couple of minutes hanging like that Aimée had become positively blue in the face. Our little guinea pig had hardly set her feet on the ground when Craig had already oiled the pulley and within five minutes we were ready to go again. We spent the entire afternoon whizzing backwards and forwards until we were exhausted.

The next morning we picked up where we had left off, when during one particularly beautiful slide, while Craig was about halfway across, the cable snapped and he fell to the ground. He fell hard onto a stone and hurt his feet, losing a few toenails in the process. He was splattered with blood, but this was the least of our problems: the Land Rover was so old that the handbrake had packed up and the car was now rolling down the hill.

Craig picked himself up and the two of us started running after the car. The scene was farcical, Craig limping along with his bleeding foot and me with my heavy prostheses; we did not stand a chance of catching the car, particularly as it was picking up speed as it went down the hill. Eventually it was brought to a halt with the help of the bushes against the fence.

With my trademark wild confidence I decided to free the car and drive it home myself, rather than ask my father for help. What need had I for help? However, getting the car out of the bushes turned out to be slightly more complex than I had imagined. Although I considered myself an expert driver and had been driving our mini Land Rover for at least two months, this time my skills were put to the test. We struggled with the car, Craig's toes turning an increasingly darker shade of red all the while, but were finally rewarded for our tenacity. I drove the car home and parked it and then went to see my father for help with Craig's foot. We told him that he had tripped over a stone in the garden — which was not that far from the truth, after all.

The experience did prompt us to stall our building plans and take some time to think and earn some pocket money, so that the next time we could buy a decent cable for our cable car-cum-slide.

The Land Rover that had so ably doubled as our crane (until the handbrake went, that is) became our main source of entertainment. It was a white 1970s model that our Uncle

Leo had lent to our father, and I used it to learn to drive when I was nine years old. To be honest, as soon as we saw it parked in my father's driveway, Carl and I were determined to get behind the wheel. It took us a while to find the keys but less time to get the hang of driving it, and before we could even see properly over the dashboard we could be found driving around the garden.

The inside of the car was old and worn but the engine was in perfect condition. I can still hear the 'dulug-dulug-dulug' noise that the engine made. I drove Carl nuts until he agreed to teach me to drive.

First he gave me a quick and basic lesson on how the mechanism behind the clutch works. In summary, he explained, the clutch separated the motor from the gear and pushing it made it possible to select a weaker but faster gear. The lower the gear the greater the grip and vice versa. Nothing new, our father had explained the workings of a car on countless different occasions. Then it was my turn. At first I was too small to see over the dashboard so I sprinted inside (I covered the 100 metres that separated us from the house and back again in under ten seconds!) and grabbed a cushion. At least with the cushion I could see in front of me and if I sat at the edge of the seat I could simultaneously touch the pedals with my prostheses.

The clutch was really stiff and the steering wheel heavy and hard. I found it difficult to engage the clutch and change gears. It was a lot to master at once. Finally I started the car, put it into gear and released my foot from the clutch as gradually as possible; slowly the car lurched forward and I was driving. I was rigid with excitement and fear as I had little clue what to do next; I had not thought that far ahead, and I tried to avoid the trees and the piles of sand. My brother was totally relaxed and enjoying the wind blowing through his hair as he appreciated the scenery, which only served to make me more nervous. Every so often he would quip, 'Check the rear-view mirror,' or an equivalent and I would rebuff him by telling him that I already had. The words were no sooner out of my mouth when — bang. I reversed into a brick wall.

I enjoyed greater success on a motorbike. I started riding when I was four years old. It was only a pedal-powered bike, but to me it was a rocket. We were still living in our Johannesburg house at the top of the hill, where there was a bit of a drop between the ground floor and the basement; the two areas were joined by a very steep staircase (the incline must have been at least 30 degrees). My favourite trick was to throw myself onto my motorbike, tummy first, and then practically propel myself rapidly down the stairs, screaming in delight. My mother had banned me from doing this but to no effect, so in despair she pretended not to see me.

Some things are simply not meant for a mother to witness.

3

The Princess and the Pugilist

When the time came for me to begin school, my parents opted for mainstream education over special-needs schooling and sent me to Constantia Kloof Primary School along with Carl.

Increasing maturity and international travel have given me an insight into my good fortune in growing up in South Africa, where the national curriculum places outdoor sporting activities on an equal footing with academic achievement and duly allocates equal time to both. I am a natural sportsman and immediately took up all the sports on offer with my customary enthusiasm, although with variable results.

Both my mother and my father encouraged our sporting activities and extra-curricular commitments. My mother considered it a priority that we each try out different sports and find something that we were good at and could continue after leaving school. Tennis had seemed the perfect option for me and so I had private tutoring. My father, on the other hand, was obsessed with gymnastics, and made it an obligatory 'hobby' for each of us. He gave us pocket money every week but required that we perform tasks for it, such as walking and feeding the dogs but also doing gymnastics. Physical training has always been integral to our lives; from about age four onwards we each had our own mini set of barbells. My first set was half a kilo, and as I grew so they became progressively heavier. My father trained with weights, and it became something we all did together. Furthermore, there were incentives for us: skipping or push-ups, abdominal exercises, the more we did the more pocket money we earned.

My paternal grandfather still works out regularly and is very fit. Now ninety-one years old and recently returned from a trip around Europe, he has his own personal gym at home and makes a point of training every day.

Cricket was nothing short of a revelation. Like most South African kids I loved cricket, and I was a good all-rounder. One particular source of joy for me with cricket was that I was exempt from having to wear those ungainly leg pads. I was especially keen on batting, and was secretly very pleased as this way I could not be penalised for being Leg Before Wicket.

While I played a lot of tennis and football, my participation in athletics was less enthusiastic. I was not a great fan. I had tried both high jump and long jump and I preferred the latter. I found high jump particularly arduous, as with my heavy prostheses it was difficult to get much lift off the ground. Carl was a swimmer but unlike him I found swimming dull.

The competitive sport that I played at club level was wrestling. My father had applied to the Amateur Wrestling Association for a dispensation allowing me to compete with prostheses, which they had granted since, unlike all-in wrestlers we were only allowed to use our upper bodies. I started when I was six years old and absolutely revelled in the sport, perhaps because it was a natural continuation of the physical way Carl and I played with one another. Carl was the epitome of assertiveness, and I was determined to earn his respect and be treated equally.

I won my first medal in wrestling. The first time you win an award is an unforgettable moment. You are enveloped in a warm buzz of emotions — pride, happiness, and the acute sense of recognition that comes with applause from your loved ones. It is addictive, almost like a drug — but a positive drug, pushing you forward to greater success. I think that if anything my prostheses probably furthered my wrestling career, since their considerable weight meant that I was solidly anchored to the ground and perhaps more stable than other competitors.

It seems odd in retrospect that running was by far my least favourite sport. Once a year our school organised an athletics day in which we all had to take part. I loathed participating as my cumbersome prostheses made the races impossibly difficult and often painful. Each year, as the dreaded athletics day neared, I tried out my forgery skills and sent a note to the teacher responsible. The teacher changed year on year, although my story usually ran broadly along the same lines:

Dear Madam,
Oscar has been unwell with the flu recently. This morning he was feeling faint. I have sent him to school anyway but think it would be better if he did not have to take part in today's athletic events. Poor child.
Thank you for your understanding.
Best regards,
Sheila Pistorius

I would then attempt my best impression of her signature, but to no avail. Inevitably the school would telephone my mother and so not only was I obliged to partake but in addition I would be punished for my misbehaviour at home.

While still at primary school I took part in numerous triathlon events (600 metres swimming, 5 kilometres running and 20 kilometres cycling). For these triathlons I had formed a team with Kaylem and Deon, two old friends I had met fishing. We had each chosen a discipline and were absolutely committed to winning our individual legs. I had chosen cycling. In our last year we triumphed and won the Junior title.

In the girls' team there was a princess; her name was Faryn Martin. We lived on the same road and our parents knew one another. She was blonde, blue-eyed and very sporty. She was a tomboy who played football with the boys and who is now part of the South African national hockey team.

As soon as I saw Faryn, I fell head over heels in love with her. I even gave her my first rose on Valentine's Day at the tender age of eight — although I must admit it took me much longer to pluck up the courage actually to speak to her. My crush lasted, unabated, until I was at least thirteen. We spent a lot of time together, playing, going to the movies or ice-skating and we always held hands. We kept in touch even after I moved to Pretoria and changed schools, and in fact we have remained close as adults. I was very happy last October when she married a wonderful guy who also happens to be a top rugby player.

She literally marked me for life. When I was about ten, we were playing football at school when she tackled me from behind, throwing her weight against my back. I ended up in the fence at the end of the field, cutting my leg in the process. You can still see the scar today and I consider it my gift from Faryn so I would never forget her.

Again, it was on her account that, aged nine, I got involved in my first fist fight — with a rival for her affections. I came off worse, but Ashton, my rival, was just lucky. Not too long after that I was involved in another more serious fight with two kids who were trying to bully me at a school function. My father did not intervene during the scuffle but that evening at home he took me to my grandfather who had been a boxing champion. Together they put me in front of the boxing punch bag and began to work on my swing. The time had come for me to learn to defend myself

46

My mother also taught me how to defend myself from unwelcome attention by using more sophisticated and less adversarial tactics. She taught me how to handle people's curiosity and how to answer their questions with ease and often with a sense of humour. Sometimes I told children that my legs were a special acquisition from Toys R Us and that if their parents worked hard enough, and saved enough money, they too could buy a pair. One of my favourite white lies was that I had lost my legs in a shark attack. Shark attacks were not unheard of in Plettenberg Bay and so my scary story was a showstopper. When I was on the beach the children would often wait for me to finish with my sandcastle and leave and then beg Carl to tell them all about the shark attack. I think my presence made them awkward and nobody wanted to hurt my feelings.

Carl was my hero and role model. He was never far from my side — my guardian angel. I remember one evening when we were on holiday. I must have been about ten years old. He found me in a bar dancing shirtless on the stage with a cigarette in my hand. At that time he smoked like a chimney but that did not stop him from yanking me off the stage and rebuking me for smoking in front of everyone. His scolding was furious and then I

47

was abruptly dispatched home.

He felt that his position as my older brother entitled him to behave this way, however much I protested. When I think back on the incident now I can only wonder what he himself was doing at the bar . . . I may have been only ten at the time, but that would have made him twelve.

One of the many advantages that came with his affection for me was that he was always prepared to keep me company, even during the interminable afternoons I spent after school at the prosthetics specialist's. Often we would spend up to three hours fitting the prostheses, making the moulds for the upper part where my stumps would sit, checking, and then trialling and adjusting each angle until they were perfect.

Carl, in true Pistorius fashion, watched the entire procedure closely. With time he became an expert trouble-shooter. He was capable of spotting the technical defects or inaccuracies that were going to create blisters and the like for me just by watching how I moved my legs and observing my gait. We were inseparable, and he was the first person I complained to or confided in. He was completely involved in my routine and often reminded me to wash my socks (sometimes washing them for me) and put talcum powder on my stumps. He drove me crazy lecturing me on how to take good care of my stumps.

Every now and again, on a Friday, our mother would come to collect us from school. Then, instead of heading home, she would take the highway: at this point we would learn that she was going to surprise us with a weekend away as a special treat. I remember adoring the tranquillity of the snow-covered Drakenberg mountains, so majestic and peaceful. We knew that she could not really afford jaunts like this, but she would put money aside specially for the purpose.

Over the years my family's financial fortunes have fluctuated significantly. I think it has been a blessing because, although my parents did their best to protect us from the brunt of it, we all now enjoy a sense of financial responsibility and respect for the value of money. As small children we lived in an enormous house and were spoilt rotten, and so when my parents divorced and we were forced to downsize we had no understanding of real hardship. From our standpoint of privileged naivety those living in apartments were destitute and our new, normal-sized house seemed very small. Fortunately there is always a constructive lesson to be drawn from these experiences.

With time we learnt to watch our pennies

and be considerate. If one of us finished school before the others we would wait for one another to avoid multiple car journeys and wasted petrol. My mother did all she could while my father's business struggled, so we tightened our belts and met our bills each month. Fortunately our paternal grandmother also contributed to our financial wellbeing.

During our early childhood my mother did not work; she helped my father but was otherwise dedicated to us. My father's bankruptcy and my parents' divorce put an end to this idyll, and for a while our finances were precarious at best. She took a part-time job which nonetheless entailed a full-time commitment, but as she started work at 7 a.m. and finished at 2 p.m. it left her free in the afternoon. She cut back wherever possible, but still managed to ensure that I received the best care and specialist attention for my prostheses and benefited wherever possible from all the latest technological advancements. I remember her baking a cake in honour of my first set of toes! We were celebrating my first prostheses that had moulded feet.

An optimist with a bubbly personality, a great sense of humour and a talent for making everything fun, my mother managed to teach us all of life's important lessons with a smile on her face. She made sure we knew that being kitted out in brand names from head to toe was of no importance — that one should never attach too much importance to such superficial considerations. It is not the make of the clothes (or how much you spend on them) that counts but how you wear them. These lessons may seem utterly commonplace, but they have remained with me and I am a better person because of them.

She was incredibly creative and always managed to do the seemingly impossible: in addition to the fun outings and holidays we had, each of us got to celebrate our birthday with a special party which always somehow remained within our budget. Our mother was actively involved in every facet of our lives, and school was no exception, where she was an active member of the Parent Teacher Association. She managed to juggle everything effortlessly (or so it seemed to us). She was dynamic and charismatic and remains an inspiration to each of us.

Although she is no longer with us, and I miss her terribly, I still feel her presence in my life. I often reread the notes that she left me. She liked to hide messages in our lunch boxes so that we would have a surprise from her during the day, things like: 'You are my special kids and I love you, Mum.' They were always beautiful words of encouragement, excerpts of poetry or passages from the Scriptures, and I have kept many of them. My mother was a devout Christian and very involved in her church, and we in turn benefited from the support of the congregation in our lives.

Throughout their divorce my parents put our serenity and wellbeing first and kept their relationship amicable and mutually respectful. They tried to shelter us from any financial hardship but as is generally the case, we children knew far more than we let on.

We lived with our mother but there were no fixed rules or enforced visitation rights. As far as was possible, we saw our father as much as we wanted to. My mother encouraged our relationship with our father, even allowing us to phone him at three in the morning if that was when we happened to feel his absence most keenly, and we needed the reassurance of speaking to him. To all intents and purposes we were still a family — all that had changed was that we stayed mainly with my mother. The only inkling we had that things were not quite as straightforward as they seemed was when we overheard inopportune family gossip as to who was to blame for the break-up. Not that we ever paid much attention to the gossip — whoever was responsible for spreading it was always speedily reprimanded and told to mind their own business.

Our parents made it their priority that we should want for nothing and continued spoiling us. My father even bought us a small boat so that we could go waterskiing. We were thrilled, as it meant that Carl and I had a whole new activity in which we could race one another and challenge each other to dares: who could spin the boat fastest, drive it the greatest distance or bounce it from the water for the longest distance. On one occasion we narrowly avoided a serious accident. We were going very fast but paying scant attention to what was going on around us, and just missed becoming caught up between two much larger vessels and their anchor lines. We would have flipped and capsized and been thrown into the water.

My mother was an extrovert who loved nothing more than laughter and spending time with friends; she always encouraged us to be outgoing. Our friendship with Neil Stevenson is a good example of her natural ease with people. Neil was a surfing champion and at the time was ranked third in the world. As kids we hero-worshipped him. My mother turned on her charm and convinced him to take me out on his board. We would see him every year and became his regular fan club. Then, in 1998, he was the victim of a shark attack in which both of his legs were viciously savaged. Incredibly he managed to pull free and swim 200 metres towards the shore with what remained of his legs dangling. He is fortunate to be alive to tell his tale because it was late in the afternoon and there was no one on the beach to hear his cries for help; he was in shock and losing a lot of blood, but somehow he held himself together and retained enough strength to swim. It was only when he pulled himself on to the beach that he realised the seriousness of his situation and how close he had come to losing his life. His doctors were forced to amputate one leg above the knee as gangrene had set in but were able to save the other leg. We have remained friends, and I like to think that his friendship with me helped to strengthen him and give him the courage not only to overcome the pain and suffering but also to continue to be actively involved in the sporting world. Today he is a champion South African paddle skier. We are both, I believe, proof of the validity of another of my mother's lessons: Never say never, and never give up. Try and try again.

My parents impressed upon us that if

something is worth doing it must be done properly. We learnt about true competitive spirit, in which the objective is not only to win. What is important is to do your best.

When we were children, our father often took us go-kart racing. My father loved racing and, because he was heavier than we were, his kart gripped the track better than ours did; on the other hand, he struggled more than we did when taking the corners. It took me years to understand that to beat him I needed to capitalise on his weakness at the corners and overtake him there. He made sure that I earned each victory. He also encouraged me to compete among my peer group. He would often invite five or six friends round and organise races. His favourite activity was to get us to race to the wall and back, with the winner being rewarded with the largest slice of cake or some such treat. Until about the age of twelve I was surprisingly agile and fast, even on my stumps (I was much lighter than I am now, of course; my body weight is now too great for the skin on my stumps to bear, despite the fact that I have had heel-skin transplanted onto the bottom of them). Often I would slip off my prostheses and sprint the distance, easily beating the competition.

4

Carpe Diem

When the time came for me to begin high school, my parents, true to form, gave me free rein. I could attend the school of my choice and so I chose Pretoria Boys' High School, an English-language boarding school with a good reputation (my father was an alumnus of the neighbouring rival Afrikaans-language school), and Carl decided to join me. Until then we had always lived in Johannesburg, and so I was keen to try somewhere new and a bit different. Pretoria seemed ideal; it was not Johannesburg, but it was only half an hour away. I was a student at Pretoria Boys' High School from 2001 until 2005, from the ages of fourteen until eighteen.

Pretoria Boys' High School was founded in 1901 and is a wonderful example of an Anglo-Saxon boarding school. Huge, magnificent pine trees flank the driveway that leads to the main school buildings. The school's architecture is imposing and grand. The school attached great value to sporting excellence, and accordingly it boasted six rugby fields, one massive and two smaller cricket pitches, an athletics track with an Astro Turfed hockey pitch at its centre (equipped with spotlights etc. for evening games) as well as two pools (one for swimming and the other for water polo), ten tennis courts and six squash courts. There was even a shooting range. The school was surrounded by verdant countryside and dramatic mountains, and effectively became my oasis. There were 1,500 pupils, of whom 400 were boarders.

I took to the place like a fish to water. I believe that people perceive you the way you perceive yourself, and as I was a happy, well-adjusted boy that is exactly how I was accepted.

A memorable incident took place on my first day of school. We were expected to line up in the entrance hall. Next to me was another new boy who at this point also knew no one. He politely introduced himself as Chris and I reciprocated. As the school's summer uniform was shorts and long socks my prostheses were obvious to all. Chris immediately enquired what had happened to me and I told him my story. Thereafter we were ordered out onto the sports field. Spontaneously he asked if I needed any help and then offered to carry my school bag — it weighed a ton and the distance to cover between our classes was pretty significant. I was gobsmacked: no one at home had ever made allowances for me in such a manner, and I found his concern not only helpful but touching. I accepted his offer, and for three weeks he carried my bag around for me. One day, however, he happened to see me, late for a class, sprinting across a field with a heavy tog bag on my shoulder! He was furious with me for having taken advantage of his kindness, but it was the start of a strong friendship that is still dear to me today.

I learnt my lesson though. Instead of me playing tricks, the other kids started playing tricks on me. The first-years shared dormitories in an army-style set-up — twenty-six boys per dormitory, with steel beds and steel cupboards all lined up next to one another. One child was in charge, based on a rota system, and it was his responsibility to keep things in order and wake everyone up in the morning.

Every evening before going to sleep I would take off my prostheses and stand them up at the foot of my bed, ready to start my day the following morning. On one occasion I awoke to agitated shouts and in my drowsy state saw flames all around. The dormitory representative was shouting that everybody must evacuate as there was a fire. I lurched for my prostheses but they were no longer where I had left them. I looked everywhere and I soon became panic-stricken. I was almost in tears, terrified that I was going to be left to die, when suddenly the fire magically disappeared and the boys came running back in laughing. They duly informed me that it was all a joke. Their prank had consisted of spraying the steel cupboards with lighter fuel and then setting fire to it. As steel does not burn, the initial effect is dramatic but the fuel is quickly consumed and the fire puts itself out. The boys in my dormitory thought their exploit was hilarious, and told me it was their way of extending a warm welcome to me.

Another favourite trick was to land me in detention for being late. I had a reputation for being a late sleeper. I studiously ignored the first and second wake-up calls every morning, which meant that by the time the third one came I had to leap out of bed practically already dressed. The hitch was that my mates would hide my legs and so the time that it took for me to find them again landed me in detention for being late. There was no end to the pranks, but as I was the originator and the victim in equal measure I revelled in them.

Indeed, I think of these games as the inevitable result of putting 150 boys together in close confinement. These experiences played a central role in bonding us as a group, and were also important in making me feel accepted on an equal footing with any of the other boys. I was a happy boarder.

For a new pupil, the first few weeks of the school year are particularly demanding and stressful. One must pass through the initiation process and become familiar with the school's routines and traditions. In addition pupils must memorise the geography of the school and the names of all the buildings and fields, the names of the teachers and, last but not least, the names of all their new schoolmates. In my opinion, all this effort is worthwhile as boarding school is such fun; there are endless new experiences to be had, as well as the pleasure of being able to spend every waking moment in the company of one's friends.

Sometimes (usually on Fridays) we would sneak out of the dormitory at night and sit by the swimming pool and chat or skinny-dip and play water polo, small pleasures that made for many memorable moments. We even smuggled our girlfriends into the dormitories. Talk about teamwork! Some of the boys had to distract the teachers on duty while the others helped the girls to get in. Saturday nights were the best fun: we would lock ourselves into one of the rooms and listen to music, chat, drink a bit and smoke.

The school colours were green, red and white. Pretoria Boys' High School boasted a Hall of Fame where it displayed all the trophies and awards won by the different champions who had passed through its gates. The awards were of two types — academic and sporting — and were then graded according to colour, half-colours going to those who played for the school's first team for an entire school year, full colours if you were part of the first team for a two-year period, and honours if you played your chosen sport at national level and wore the Springbok colours. The awards were also worn in the school uniform: for example, full colours entitled you to a school blazer with a wide red and green stripe around it. I was awarded full sporting colours in 2004 and honours in 2005.

At the apex of the school's student body were the prefects. They were our elite, consisting of the best thirty or so boys in the last year of school, and were responsible for leadership in the school as well as activities like fund-raising and the organisation of certain events. In addition, each prefect was assigned to a dormitory (approximately three to each). As an incentive the prefects were entitled to special perks and concessions — it was considered a reward for their added involvement in the school and for having demonstrated their commitment to follow the school ethic and discipline.

Pretoria Boys' High taught its pupils to respect one another and respect the traditions of the school. It gave us a sterling education. Pride in our school and appreciation of our good fortune at being part of this illustrious family were instilled in us, and as a consequence we learnt to take care of our external appearance and keep our uniforms clean and tidy. We understood that we were the face of the school, and that our behaviour and appearance reflected that; it was important that the school protected its good reputation and therefore that people were suitably impressed by us.

The raising of the flag marked the beginning of every day, while every afternoon at half past five, one pupil would go up into the school tower to lower the flag and play 'The Last Post', a relic of a bygone, more military-style education. At that moment, wherever you were in the school, whatever you happened to be doing, you were obliged to stand to attention, put your hand over your heart and observe two minutes' silence. The respect for this rule was absolute and applied to all, even our sporting opponents. No matter where you were, in the thick of a rugby match or a water polo game, everything would come to an immediate halt.

Like other schools of this ilk, Pretoria Boys' High has its own chant, which was used as a war cry in sporting events to encourage and support our teams. We were taught to respect ourselves and one another and to be disciplined. We could play hard but we had also to work hard. The school's objective was to produce both well-educated and well-rounded young gentlemen.

Pretoria Boys' High taught by example and inspiration, setting out to show you that you were no longer a child but a young man, and that with the opportunity came a certain responsibility. Corporal punishment is illegal in South African schools, but on occasion people did turn a blind eye. At our school the prefects were in charge of discipline; the teaching staff trusted them completely, confident in the knowledge that they too had been through the school system and were worthy young men who would not abuse their position of power.

Standard Six, the beginning of your school career and your time as a boarding pupil at

Pretoria Boys' High School, is marked by a couple of important rites of passage. For the first three weeks none of the students are allowed to leave the premises to go home. This is a special time that is dedicated to getting to know the school and your new friends, prefects and teachers. We were obliged to learn all students' and prefects' names, and any mistakes in this regard were immediately punished. It was a powerful incentive. There were two principal types of punishment, called *obstan*, which is the Afrikaans word for 'wake up': they were given this name as they were detached from the school and you were obliged to do them out of hours, i.e. first thing in the morning before you went to school. The first, more traditional punishment consisted of having to write a thousand words on a given topic, while the second was decidedly more physical. The prefect in charge would wake you up before sunrise — at approximately four thirty in the morning — and make you run for two and a half hours. You were forced to run for 50 metres, drink something, roll around on the ground and then repeat the whole procedure all over again. I can tell you from experience it is an awful punishment.

Another favourite was to make you run the 50 metres with another boy sitting on your shoulders and then swap you around and so on. At the end you were absolutely exhausted and could hardly stand. Another much-loved punishment was to make you run 400 metres with two bricks on your head in under two minutes and fifteen seconds, otherwise you had to start all over again. Of course it was impossible: the more tired you became the more chance you had of dropping the bricks and the slower you went. The genius behind the punishment was in setting the time limit according to the slowest child. If the slowest child did not make it everyone had to start again. It was a surreptitious way of getting children to care about one another and particularly of getting them to work together and help the weakest link. At the end of these sessions we were all shattered and desperate to go back to bed, but by then it was time for school. Luckily, at that age your strength returns quite quickly.

I found the written punishment more difficult than the physical ones. The prefect in charge would write a topic on the blackboard, but we were forbidden to name the topic in the thousand words we were required to write. The more absurd the topic the better, for example 'The Six Lives of a Ping Pong Ball' or 'The Story of the Mongolian Mouse and the Turtle'. A further dimension to the punishment which proved popular with the prefects was to oblige us to write every fifth line in Chinese — a nice touch, but impossible for most of us. My worst punishment ever was being ordered to 'Describe an object that is colourless, odourless and shapeless without using any of these words'. To complicate matters the prefects actually read our essays, and so if we made a mistake or went off the topic, or were a bit too smart, we would then be given two thousand words to complete for the next day. It was a no-win situation.

Sometimes the prefects punished us with the equivalent of community service. We had to stay indoors and paint the doors, sand the tables, or carry out any leftover tasks that needed to be completed. I far preferred physical punishment to the other types of task.

Every year, the eve of our first day at school was reserved for the Standard Six 'Walking the Table'. The event took place in our Honours Hall, which was formerly the dining room and still boasts long tables with benches alongside them. All the boys crowd into the room and then line one of the long tables on either side. The new kids — the Standard Six children — then make their entrance one by one and are obliged, alone, to walk barefoot the length of the table. It is a frightening moment, as you are a newcomer and know no one. Once you get to the end of the table you are instructed to tell a joke, but this, it turns out, merely prolongs the mockery at your expense: no one laughs, and once you have been duly informed that your jokes are rotten you are asked to try harder or to lift your T-shirt and show off your muscles. If you refuse the other boys jump onto and around the table and scare you witless threatening you (I am sure you can imagine the noise that 150 boys can make crowding around a table). I found the experience terrifying, but thereafter you are accepted as one of them into dormitory life.

In order to mark their arrival at the senior school, all the Standard Six boys go away together on a camping weekend at the beginning of the year. It is an initiation into the ways of the school. The prefects have free rein and they certainly put us through the mill. We were woken up in the middle of the night as they screamed at us and then drenched us with buckets of freezing water. I remember one boy who had a broken leg in a cast being chucked into the swimming pool as he confused some of the lyrics while singing the school hymn. It was wild.

We were all in tears and pleading to go

home. I remember the older boys yelling at us and asking us who we thought we were. Did we think we were adults? Did we think we were young men? 'Make a point of watching your step, young boy. This is serious, respect the rules because if you don't you will be punished!' They set us all sorts of different tests: one was an obstacle course, while another involved being dropped off in a field seemingly in the middle of nowhere, equipped with nothing but a compass, the task being to work your way back to the camp within a certain time frame. It was really tough, but in my opinion the experience was character-building.

I was still a lightweight at that age and I found the older boys terrifying. The rough language and abrasive approach were so intimidating. Some of them were huge burly rugby players who weighed up to 100 kilos; to us they seemed almost superhuman.

In my last year in the dormitory I became responsible for the first-year students. They slept in dormitories of twenty children per room, with a small adjoining room with a cupboard and a desk for the person overseeing them. Lights out was nine o'clock, but they were allowed to talk to one another until ten, when silence became obligatory. On the whole the children were well behaved and respectful of the rules, and always generously shared with me the endless supply of treats their mothers sent to them. Mothers have a tendency to spoil their sons rotten when they first leave home.

Over and above taking care of the dormitory the older children were expected to mentor the younger children and look out for them generally. In principle the older boy must advise and support the younger, and should be there to help him should he experience any problems or difficulties at school. This system of mentoring, also known as fagging or skivvying, has plenty of advantages for the older child as well. I remember with great affection a little boy called Allan Burnett who was my skivvy. He used to sleep closest to my door; if I became hungry during the evening or when I was studying late, all I had to do was call his name and he would wake up and bring me a coffee with cookies. When I needed to stay up late to study but found myself falling asleep, I would wake him. We would chat a bit, I would have a break and a snack, and then he could go back to bed and I would continue studying. In return I was responsible for Allan: I helped him with his homework wherever possible and went to support him when he played in sports matches. Many schools no longer use the fagging system, but

I think it is a fantastic way to mentor children, ensuring that they have the support of someone who has already been through the same experiences. It is a little like having a big brother. Of course, one has to make sure that the system is not abused, but when it is correctly and sensitively handled I think there are significant advantages for everyone involved.

5

The Coldest Summer

In my first year at Pretoria Boys' High I played cricket. I was eager to try rugby but slightly apprehensive as I had never played before (my junior school had not had a rugby field). By my second year I had grown in confidence, so I decided to substitute rugby and water polo for cricket and tennis and I have never looked back. I did not do athletics, but loved long-distance running. My preferred distance was 10 kilometres, and I was helped by the fact that I was using much lighter prostheses. Chris Hatting, a friend of my father's, designed the prostheses. Chris was an aeronautical engineer obsessed with design; he had begun to produce the prostheses towards the end of 2001. They were handcrafted, relatively short and shaped like hooks; as they were still at a fairly early stage of development they frequently broke, but I used them until at least June 2004.

Pretoria Boys' High hosted a range of endurance races: one was called 'The Ten Kilometre Classic', another 'the King of the Mountains'. I was very competitive and generally finished within the top ten or fifteen in the school. I had become very fit as I cycled a lot. While I lived at my father's I often cycled to school and back, a distance of 24 kilometres. I was never part of the school cross-country team, but the only reason for this was the importance the sporting officials at the school placed on focus and training: they believed that it was more important truly to excel in one or two chosen sports than to be merely good at five or six sports. Excellence was their priority, and indeed by my penultimate year at the school three boys had qualified for national level athletics, five were playing in the Springbok under-nineteens rugby team and many more were playing at provincial level. We were semi-professional sportsmen, not just all-rounders. My strengths were rugby and water polo, to which I was totally committed. I was continually striving to better my achievements.

I adored rugby and thoroughly enjoyed playing it. I was never shy to exploit the fact that some boys were nervous or frightened of my prostheses. I remember one match that I played in Johannesburg: I was running with the ball and my opponent was nervous of tackling me, but eventually he pushed me forward and I duly fell over and lost a leg in the process. I just carried on as I was determined to keep the ball in play, and so I hopped over the line, but this guy kept on pushing me. This time I punched him, drawing applause from my friends, and then put my prostheses back on and calmly scored a try. I really savoured that moment of victory and was delighted when the coach scolded my opponent for his behaviour.

Running was part of my rugby training. In addition to your chosen sports training programme, Pretoria Boys' High had four obligatory track races per week. There were always boys milling around the dormitories who did not have sport that day or who had already finished training, and at such moments we were all packed off to the tracks to practise running. Our school's sporting routine was intense but without doubt it produced some fine athletes. My rugby team, for example, was made up entirely of boarders, and this was probably because the training was so hard and concentrated that it was much easier to live on the school grounds; boarding also gave the pupils ready access to all the useful material support.

In November 2001 my mother remarried.

At first my mother's decision hit my brother Carl really hard. She had always promised that she would never remarry unless she met the perfect man and even then she would do so only with our consent. For many years she had been as good as her word, despite a steady flow of suitors through the door. She was a real lady, and her views were traditional in just about every respect: she would never have agreed to live with someone or have them stay over, since for her it was important to do things properly, for which I have always respected her. We were already living at boarding school by this point, and so I was completely taken by surprise when, without any warning, she took us aside and told us her plans. Carl felt betrayed, and his initial reaction was to storm out in fury, leaving my mother in tears. Aimée and I felt rather awkward to begin with, but we were soon reconciled to the idea of her remarrying: we were happy to know that somebody was making her happy. In Carl's opinion, when our parents divorced he became the man of the house and responsible for our wellbeing; the fact that our mother had not made him party to this important change in her life left him feeling slighted. Fortunately for all of us, although Carl can be hot-headed and tends to be frank in the expression of his opinion, he isn't a man to dwell on life's problems, and so by the time of our mother's wedding he had come round to the idea and understood her decision. In fact, he took my mother's new husband — a pilot by profession — to his heart and to this day they remain close friends.

The summer after their wedding, and again without warning, my mother fell ill and was hospitalised. Her illness was virulent and complicated by an initial misdiagnosis. Her health deteriorated extremely rapidly and she passed away just one month later. The doctors initially diagnosed her with hepatitis. Carl had been ill with it not long before, and she was showing similar symptoms. When the treatment brought her no relief it became clear that they had to do further tests; however, by the time the correct diagnosis was made it was too late.

During her stay at the hospital we would often be summoned by friends and relatives telling us that she had taken a turn for the worse and that we should come to the hospital, but each time this happened she seemed to pull through and begin to recover. These false alarms happened so often that we eventually became inured to them; it never occurred to us that she might not get better.

I remember the day my mother died very clearly. It was 6 March 2002. I have since had this date tattooed alongside her birth date on my arm, my only tattoos. That day I was at school in a history lesson when the school principal interrupted the class to tell me I had ten minutes to collect my things; my father would be waiting for me at the school gate. Carl and I arrived at the gate just in time to witness my father driving his enormous Mercedes towards us at breakneck speed. It was clear that something was not right: he was shouting at us to hurry up and get in, and seemed to be on the verge of tears. Although my parents had been divorced for years they still felt great affection for one another. All of our closest friends and family were at the hospital, and it became increasingly obvious that this day was different and that my mother was very close to death. We were rushed into her room to be by her side, and ten minutes later she left us.

It was a very distressing moment. She could no longer recognise us as she had slipped into a coma, and she was heavily intubated as her organs were failing. It broke my heart to see her this way. She no longer looked like herself.

Initially I thought I handled her death pretty well. I was the only one who was not crying and I helped to comfort my brother and sister. After the funeral I decided to return to school. I told everyone I was fine, but what I did not realise was that I was desperate to get back into my routine and to a world where my days were structured. Only a few of my classmates knew about my loss; this suited me, as it kept the questions to a minimum. Everything seemed under control, but then I woke up the next morning in floods of tears. I had completely lost my bearings. I went to stay with a friend for a couple of days as I had lost all interest in my school environment. I would then recover my composure and return to school, only to be stricken by my grief once again and have to go and stay with someone else. It was awful.

Sport was my salvation, as it helped me to get through this difficult time. My mother had been a strong woman, the centre of my world. Sporting activity was the only thing which could distract me from such a loss.

After our mother's death we spent weekends at our Aunt Diane's house. Diane is my mother's sister, and Aimée lived with her while she finished school in Johannesburg. For a couple of years, Carl and I were rather like rudderless boats — effectively homeless, floating between boarding school,

Diane's house and the houses of our closest friends.

Carl and I used to run together. He was faster than me, but he would encourage me endlessly and spur me on. Carl has always had a soft spot for extreme sports. Even when we were boys he used to make fun of my playing cricket, asking me what on earth was keeping me on a sports pitch when I could be canoeing down rivers or waterskiing. His first love was, and remains to this day, motor racing.

In the months following my mother's death we became keen to assert our independence. As a result, when Carl was still only seventeen he bought his first car. I thought it was a beautiful car — a small white Golf, in which he had made a point of installing a fantastic sound system. We were elated to be free (or almost, as in South Africa eighteen is the legal age for a driving licence). I was only fifteen, but every now and then Carl, being the fantastic big brother that he is, allowed me to drive around the streets of Pretoria with the music blaring.

Nothing could have prepared me for my next traumatic, life-changing event. On 21 June 2003 I was playing rugby when I was tackled with what is commonly called a 'hospital pass'. I never even saw it coming. A hospital pass is a high pass that earned its particular name from the high probability that it would land you in a plaster cast or even a hospital bed. I was playing on the wing. A high ball came my way, and as I stopped and then jumped to catch it, I was tackled from either side by two enormous players. They simply slammed into me, one on the left and one on the right. I felt a sharp pain, and when my body finally hit the ground I saw that my left leg was sticking out all askew. It did not look good, but I assumed (or hoped) that it was just my prosthesis. At least they were relatively easy to fix.

As you may know, rugby in South Africa is more a religion than a sport. Fathers pass their teams down to their sons and it is all taken very seriously. The majority of the fathers come to watch the matches, and so there is often a beer tent by the field. They can drink as they egg their sons on, and inevitably they often become rowdy and boisterous. That afternoon one of the spectators started goading me to stand up and 'stop behaving like a girl'. Not wishing to be seen as a sissy, I pulled myself up but was in a lot of pain. Somehow I managed to finish the match and pedal the 6 kilometres home. The next day I woke up with a very swollen and bruised knee. I could hardly move, and soon found myself back in the care of Gerry Versveld. It looked like my sporting days were over. I was only sixteen.

6

The First Time

So there I was, back in Gerry Versveld's office. We had never lost touch, but it had been a while since we had last seen one another, and he knew nothing of my sporting successes. When I told him that I had hurt myself playing rugby he was astounded and burst out laughing. My morale was low, and I could not see what there was to smile about.

Gerry was able to heal me without the need for any surgical intervention, and he further reassured me that if I followed instructions and respected my rehabilitation process of low-intensity gym workouts and aerobic training in water, I would soon be able to return to sport. After three long months of enforced inaction and rest, I began my physiotherapy at the Sports Science Institute, which is part of the University of Pretoria. I was placed in the care of Heinrich Nolte, who advised me to concentrate on sprinting, which is apparently the best way to regain functionality in the knee joint. He put me in touch with Ampie Louw, who was coaching athletics at university level. I was sceptical about the arrangement as I had never had an affinity for athletics, and I even tried to pull out, but was duly informed by Nolte (whose opinion was supported by all my sporting heroes) that if I wanted to be ready and perform in the next rugby season (which was due to begin the following April), I needed to do as instructed and start sprint training. I acquiesced, and my training with Ampie began on 1 January 2004.

At the start of that year I was still using the handcrafted prostheses made by our family friend Chris Hatting. They were less expensive than the mass-produced equivalents but they were brittle and temperamental, breaking very easily. Living in South Africa meant we had very limited access to the more technologically advanced prostheses designed for sportspeople, but one advantage was that I was the equivalent of a guinea pig for Chris, and he designed my prosthetics with my specific needs in mind. His talent was such that in 2003 he was headhunted by an American firm and went to live and work in America. In June 2004 he invited me to fly to the USA and trial their new brand of prostheses, known as Cheetahs. Cheetahs, first produced in the late 1990s, are probably the most popular prosthetic limb on the market. Constructed from carbon fibre, they give their users unprecedented freedom because of their particular combination of durability and lightness. Ever since that first trial Cheetahs have been my running legs.

When I began training with Ampie my sole objective was to qualify for my rugby team, but gradually I found myself developing a taste for athletics. I realised that the main reason I had hated it as a young child was because of my heavy prostheses — they weighed more than 3 kilos each — which made running incredibly difficult. The weight of the prostheses helped me develop muscle tone but made me cumbersome, whereas with the Cheetahs, which were about half the weight, athletics suddenly became fun and I began to think I might be able to achieve something.

Three weeks into my training programme, on 28 January, I took part in my first 100-metre race. My favourite teacher, Mrs Miller, had decided to register me for the race. Mrs Miller was one of my greatest fans, a charming and rather eccentric woman who, particularly after my mother's passing, took a great interest in my life. She even took it upon herself to counsel me about my romantic interests. At one of our school dances, after a row with my then girlfriend, I retreated to a corner alone. She noticed my maudlin behaviour and came to reassure me that all would right itself. She even topped it off by hugging me in front of everyone. My friends really took me to task about that one.

On this occasion she had taken the initiative of telephoning the organisers of the race in Bloemfontein to enquire whether they would allow an athlete running on prostheses to compete. She had met with a lukewarm reaction, but her faith in me made her persistent, and eventually she managed to bring them round. I think they all expected me to come last, but as it turned out I won the race easily. It was an incredible experience. All the spectators — people representing all the different schools — were on their feet shouting my name and applauding. To add to my delight, I was also part of the school's relay team. I ran the last leg, and my performance clinched the trophy for my school.

My father was watching me and was riveted by my performance. I had not seen him as excited and energised in a long time. He was jumping up and down, repeating to all who would listen to him: 'Oscar completed the 100 metres in 11.72! That's incredible, that's a really good time!'

As soon as we got home he started phoning all his closest friends to tell them about my achievement. At first I was touched at his elation and amused by his pride, but once his friends started calling to congratulate me I told him he had overstepped the mark. I thought my father was exaggerating. That evening he, ever the stubborn Pistorius, spent his time researching on the internet and compiling information about disabled athletes, comparing my time with that of other athletes in this category. At the time we knew absolutely nothing about the Paralympics. He discovered that I would be classified as a T43, the category which covers bilateral amputees, and to our collective amazement he read that my time, 11.72 for 100 metres, was in fact a new world record. Until then the record had stood at 12.20.

From that moment things started to move very quickly. Using Chris's prostheses, within the month I had improved my time from 11.72 to 11.51, breaking my own world record in the process. Then, following Ampie's encouragement and advice, I decided to compete in the South African Disabled Games. It was a first for me. Until then I had had no contact whatsoever with the world of disabled athletics and the experience of it made me approach my sporting career from a completely different perspective. I found it quite an odd experience: I felt very isolated and detached from the event, since not only did I know no one but I was still focused on returning to my career in rugby, and so I made little effort to participate. I would arrive, warm up, race and immediately leave. I did not feel that I belonged.

In truth, I had other things on my mind. I had fallen in love for the first time and my girlfriend, Nandi, was a ball of fire. I could not keep up with her as she kept changing her mind. One minute she was interested in me, the next she was less certain. She was great fun but I needed more consistency and so decided to break up. Hot on Nandi's heels love struck for real. It was May 2004 and along with a friend I decided to organise a big lunch party. Each of us had to invite ten people whom the other did not know, and he invited a girl called Vicky. I was smitten at first sight. She was beautiful, charming and unusual. We immediately hit it off and talked for hours, and later that evening I met up with her at a bonfire-night party. We were in love. As it was not long before our annual school ball I asked her to accompany me but unfortunately she had already agreed to attend the dance in the company of a friend of mine. If I had not been so disappointed it would have been amusing. Raul, the friend in question, and I had been waxing lyrical to one another about our new love interests who shared the name Vicky . . . Little did we know we were talking about the same person. The evening passed in an embarrassing blur with us staring doe-eyed at one another, and pretty much as soon as the midnight bell rang and the ball was over Vicky and I started going out. We remained together for the next two years.

In the meantime Carl had finished school and went off to work. It became almost impossible for him to keep up with my engagements and ferry me back and forth between my sporting commitments and training sessions, and so I decided to buy myself a car. I had saved quite a bit of money that I had earned by participating in a television advertisement, and in addition I received a monthly bursary from MacSteel, the company that produced the carbon prostheses I was using at the time. They considered it a contribution to my sports training. I started trawling the car dealers but fortunately about a week into my search a friend of my father's came to my aid, explaining that he could help me buy a car through the company that he worked for.

And so it was that in May 2004 I bought my first car. It was marvellous, a Smart cabriolet in black and silver; I remember absolutely everything about it, and rather in the same way that your first love remains special to you, so this car will always have a place in my heart. I have many wonderful memories of that car, but the overriding feeling it gave me — one that remains with me to this day — was the sense of freedom that came with owning my first car. It was exactly as I had dreamed, and my ultimate pleasure was to take it out at night and drive on the freeway with the music on loud and the wind in my hair.

I was training very hard at this time, and after my performance at the South African Disabled Games I was informed that, after only eight months of athletics, I had been chosen to represent South Africa at the Paralympics in Athens 2004. I was terrified at the thought of competing against some of today's sporting legends, like the Americans Brian Frasure and Marlon Shirley — monolateral amputees and therefore potentially much more powerful than me. Athletics was still new to me (I had not yet learnt to use the starting blocks correctly) and I did not feel ready to compete on the international stage.

In rugby, when you run your body is in a

state of alertness and you are conditioned to be aware of what is happening on the entire field. You watch the other players, calibrate the distances between you and watch carefully for any gaps or changes in the rhythm of the play. Athletics is the exact opposite. In athletics you need to be absolutely focused within yourself: indeed, were it not for the fact you need to see to keep within your lane it would be better to run with your eyes shut. Peripheral vision only serves to distract you, detracting from the energy and focus you need to win.

Rugby is a very physical game: you are in a state of perpetual tension waiting and watching for your opponents to move. Your entire body is required as you scrum, tackle, jump, score and run. In athletics it is vital to relax: I found this very difficult and had to work at it considerably. While I was at the Athens Paralympics a journalist asked me why I was chewing gum. The truth is that it helps me to relax. I find it loosens my jaw, which is a great help — to run well you need to loosen your jaw and neck in order to facilitate movement in the shoulders. My coach is forever reminding me: Relax, Oscar. Initially relaxation seemed to me to be a contradiction in terms — how can you relax at the very moment you are required to run as fast as you possibly can? But slowly I have come to understand the thought process behind this.

Posture is also of paramount importance, and I am still working at perfecting mine. Take Maurice Greene, the great American sprinter: when he begins a race, he pushes from the block with his legs spread far apart and then he gradually narrows the distance between his feet. As he is very fast I thought I should try to imitate his style, but of course the way in which you run is determined by your size, weight and frame. For a shorter athlete, the choppy style adopted by Maurice Greene is very powerful, but for a taller athlete that same style will simply cause him to waste energy and lose speed accordingly. As an athlete you need to calibrate the technique and elegance of movement with the energetic yield of the sprint so as to obtain maximum speed and therefore results. The more aggressive or tense you are the more energy you waste. You need to be calm and in harmony with yourself to feel the moment that your foot touches the ground and then judge the instant at which you must again push forward.

I have also had to learn to use my arms. To be honest I still struggle with the concept of the kinetic chain, which means simply that everything is connected. In other words, if you push your pelvis forward your bottom will stick out and so you will lose momentum. This is known technically as being seated, and it prevents you from developing speed. You need to pull your pelvis inward and bring your spine forward. These may seem tiny adjustments (sometimes it is just a millimetre forwards or backwards), but they make all the difference.

I struggle with the initial part of the race. The weakest element of my sprinting is the point at which I am ready to go, bent over with my feet on the blocks. Your body follows your head, and as I am a naturally inquisitive person I like to look around me. The instant the gun goes and the race begins I look up too quickly, and so my back straightens too soon. I have to concentrate on keeping my head down for at least the first 30 metres of the race so that I keep my body in the correct position, straightening my back gradually without any brusque movements. I am still working at this as I know there is much room for improvement, but with Ampie's help I am sure I will get there.

Ampie is an excellent coach. With me he uses the 'zones method', a sporting technique made famous by Michael Johnson. When I race, I do a lot of stretching during my warm-up, then I enter the first 'zone': I relax by deep breathing and by visualising the race in my mind. It is as though I am mentally programming myself, as I map out the points at which I need to accelerate, others where I need to conserve energy, and then the stretch in which I have to give the race everything I have got. Once I have accomplished this mental preparation I put it aside. It is time to move into the next 'zone': at this point I prepare my starting blocks. I adjust them and balance them until I am certain that they are perfect. Then I move away.

As I have said, initially I really struggled with the starting blocks. To help me out Ampie agreed with the race starter (who has since become a friend) that I should be allowed to begin on my feet and not the blocks. But even then I struggled to stay still: I fidgeted too much and so inevitably got off to a bad start. If you are not crouched with your feet on the blocks your initial push-off lacks coordination and is significantly less energy-efficient. I have worked very hard to master the blocks but I know that I have not conquered them yet as I am still not entirely comfortable and at ease.

No athlete manages a perfect start at every race. It is an ongoing process, but I have found it particularly difficult not only because

I am not used to being in that position, but also because I cannot feel the blocks as I do not have feet. However, I have learnt an immense amount with Ampie. He has taught me to position my body correctly, basically by crouching down but with my body slanted forwards as the gun goes off, ensuring that I spring off: this enables me to gain up to 40 centimetres over the duration of the race. As you wait for the gun to go, it is important to push your feet into the blocks, as this will increase the drive behind you as you push off at the start of the race.

Returning to my 'zones', once I have checked that the blocks are correctly positioned in the ground and will not slip then all is ready, and it is time to wait for the race to begin. In my opinion this is the most stressful moment: you know that you need to relax but your mind is racing with anxiety and concerns about the other competitors. The next 'zone' is when you are ready to race. You must be concentrated but calm. Competitive, but focused only on the lane in which you will race, not on your competitors or the general excitement around you.

I am the kind of athlete who performs better when running from behind. In short, I prefer chasing to leading and so I try to avoid the eighth running lane where you are out in front of everyone else. I like the first three lanes, since that way I always have someone in front of me to chase. It motivates me as I push myself to catch the person and overtake them. It helps me to give my best at the end of the race.

But in the moment before the race begins, when you are squatting down with your feet on the blocks you need to inhale deeply a couple of times and then hold your breath. It is vital that instead of waiting for the noise of the gun that starts the race you concentrate on your movement. Many athletes are so focused on the sound of the gun that when it eventually goes off they remain immobile for a fraction of a second. It is almost as though they have forgotten what the gun signals and so they waste precious seconds. Instead, it is better to assume something resembling a trance-like state, in which you remind yourself that you are ready to run and that it is the noise of the gun that will signal when you can go. That way you are concentrated on the moment you propel yourself forwards and not on the noise itself. It may seem a small difference, but it will make you mentally stronger and faster on the track.

From a strictly personal perspective, it is

crucial for me to have a technique to help me cope with the enormous psychological pressure that comes with the competition and the racing environment. I found the nervous tension that is inherent in the build-up to a race hard to handle. On the day before a race I am often so nervous that I am physically nauseous. I want to race but all my fears and self-doubt resurface and I am a jittering wreck. On the day of the race itself I always find twenty good excuses why I can't race — I am not up to it, I have a stiff neck or I slept badly — nothing really important, but still I have to mentally work myself towards a healthy competitive state. Yet once I cross the finishing line, all I want to do is start the whole process all over again. I believe that if you can channel this nervous energy it can work to your advantage. Many athletes contend that nervous tension is simply proof of your ambition.

I will never forget my 200-metre race at the Paralympics in Athens. There I was on my starting blocks, racing in lane number seven, surrounded by athletes who were both much older and much more experienced than me. In the sixth lane was Brian Frasure, the reigning World Champion, while in the eighth was a French athlete called Dominique André who during his warm-up began grunting and spitting. I found his behaviour both disturbing and nerve-racking. I could not concentrate (which in hindsight was probably exactly the point of his behaviour). I was completely intimidated. I was only seventeen years old and a newcomer at that. To complicate matters there were four false starts. When the gun marking the fifth start sounded, I froze. I had convinced myself that it was going to be another false start, and when it was not I was so taken by surprise that I was immobilised. It was horrible — by the time I realised that the second shot was never coming I was already 1.8 seconds behind the others. In retrospect my confusion was one of the things that made my performance in that race so special to me. I ran for all I was worth, managed to catch the pack, and went on to win the gold medal. Marlon Shirley and Brian Frasure came respectively second and third. My time (21.97) set a new world record, which I have since improved on. It is hard to describe my emotion — it was an incredible achievement and a great triumph.

It is astounding to think back on that moment of my life: so much has happened since that it seems a lifetime ago. When I look at the photographs of me on the winner's podium with the laurel leaves around my head and gold medal around my neck I am struck by how young I look.

The Athens Paralympics were a fantastic experience. The Olympic Village was mindboggling: it was 4,000 square metres in size and the food hall boasted the capacity to feed 16,000 people simultaneously and at any time of day or night. There was no limit to what you could eat: the choice went right across the culinary spectrum. Even McDonald's had a counter that was 30 metres long, and all this was entirely free for the athletes. As we were in Greece, the fruit was delicious and plentiful. Once I had finished my races I went straight to McDonald's, ordered five Big Macs and proceeded to devour them one after the other. Pre-race Big Macs are of course strictly prohibited, but once I was finished I gave myself free rein.

The Olympic Village also hosted two entertainment zones, each equipped with huge TV screens and PlayStation points with all the Olympic sports available. By the end of the week athletes had blisters on their hands from their devotion to PlayStation and the intense competitiveness with which they had been playing the games. It was a serious business. There were electronic kiosks dispensing a seemingly endless supply of ice creams and cool drinks. Athletes had an electronic card system that allowed them to order and consume whatever they wanted for free. It was amazing.

Once the Games were over I toured the Greek islands — Mykonos, Paros, to name only two; there were so many I can barely recall them all. It was a magical experience for me as I slept on the beaches by night and by day toured my chosen island by Vespa.

But it wasn't just the beauty of the location or the incredible facilities of the Olympic Village that made this a life-changing experience for me. It opened my eyes to a world that I had previously been disdainful of. I began to understand that by participating solely in able-bodied sport, I was depriving myself; I had never before enjoyed similar levels of sporting camaraderie and sportsmanship. Disabled sport is equally competitive — after all, it is a competition between serious, dedicated athletes — but a unique atmosphere of profound mutual respect prevails. I came to regret having come to disabled sport so late, and in particular to races between amputee athletes. At the highest level the difference between the qualifying times and the winning times and between each of the athletes is so slim that each competitor has to push him — or herself to the limit. We are driven by the desire for victory and the pursuit of excellence. But once the race is over we can all go out for dinner together and enjoy the camaraderie, understanding and friendship.

While in Athens I had the good fortune to meet an extraordinary athlete who has changed my approach to my accomplishments for ever. A couple of days before a race, I decided to attend a swimming event — I think it was the 200 metres butterfly — when I noticed one swimmer, whose time was double that of the other athletes. He was competing although he was without one arm and both legs. He seemed to be completely oblivious to the other swimmers. After the race I went to speak to him because I wanted to tell him that I had found his performance remarkable. I was wearing shorts, so my prostheses were visible. We chatted a bit and he asked what my speciality was. I replied that I was a sprinter and that it was the first time I had participated in such an important disabled event. He told me that he could see nothing 'disabled' in his performance. It made no difference to him as he was not competing against the other athletes — he was competing against himself and his goal was to improve his time. He struck a profound chord with me: his perspective exactly mirrored my own, and I too share this approach to sporting excellence.

When people ask me why I want to compete in the Olympics when I cannot be sure of qualifying for the semi-finals or the finals I try to explain that they are missing the point. It is a point which applies equally to the Paralympics. The prime objective is not to compete against other athletes. Of course it is fantastic to win, but however sweet the moment of victory may be, it is far preferable to come second or third but better your own personal best time than come first with a time that is slower than your personal best. What I learnt while participating in Athens is that what is really important is not the victory over your adversaries but the victory over your own limitations. This, in my opinion, is the essence of true sporting endeavour and it is the absence of this outlook that lies at the heart of problems such as the doping scandals that have plagued professional sport.

People often ask me why I want to participate in the Olympic Games and whether it is because I consider the Paralympics second-best. I believe the two games are not mutually exclusive. It is not because I am able to compete in the

Olympics that I will not compete in the Paralympics. To me the Olympics are just another sporting avenue, and like most other athletes I am eager to explore every possibility and to be present and competitive in all the top sporting arenas. I do not consider the Paralympics to be inferior, merely different, and it remains incontestable that the Olympics are the ultimate sporting event.

I am not a Paralympic athlete, nor am I an Olympic athlete. I am simply an athlete and a sprinter.

7

One of a Kind?
Normal versus
Special

Unbeknownst to me, my victory and my status as gold medallist at the Athens Paralympics 2004 had changed my life for ever. I became a sporting celebrity overnight and the media interest and the angle they chose elevated me to a superhero for disabled people worldwide.

My return to South Africa was particularly stressful for me. I had not actually grasped the significance of having my name in all the newspapers; suddenly journalists were queuing up to interview me. Initially I was euphoric, but by November I was burnt out by the combination of intensive training and racing and the press attention. I decided to take a holiday and headed to the coast with my family for a month and a half.

The changes in my life had been drastic and sudden but I gradually got used to a new equilibrium in my life. When I first shot to fame I was both young and naive, and found myself taking interviews with journalists very personally and getting particularly upset when the results were less than flattering or my words were taken out of context. With time I have come to understand that each of us has a job and a role to fulfil and that the journalists cannot only write from one perspective. Now, through the interviews I give, my principal aim is to contribute towards changing people's attitudes and perception of Paralympic sport.

While in London in 2007 for a press conference, I took issue with what is, in my opinion, the double standards applied by much of the press while reporting on Paralympic sports. In able-bodied sporting events, when athletes underperform — even if they win — they are called to account by the press. Their slower time is scrutinised, and journalists conjecture on their lack of general fitness, wondering whether this is due to inadequate training, a recent injury or some other cause. In Paralympics this rarely happens. However mediocre the performance, or poor the race time, the press comment only on how wonderful the sportsmanship was or what remarkable endurance or competitive spirit was displayed by the athletes. I have asked myself on countless occasions why it is that the press feel that Paralympic athletes cannot be treated like the serious athletes they are and called to account for the level of their performance, simply because they are disabled? If your time is slower than your previous times — even in victory — or your performance is less impressive, being called to account will serve to motivate you as an athlete and encourage you to better your performance on each fresh occasion. To say that you won the race but that you did not realise your full potential is hardly an insult — it should be considered encouraging.

Although I have not been part of the Paralympic sporting world for long, I feel that people are too ready to confine any comment to the symbolic side of Paralympic competition. In the main, we hear only about the inspirational stories of people who have overcome obstacles and hardship to compete. I am not for one minute suggesting that it is not important to spread the word of these important accomplishments, but in no way should this negate applying normal standards of excellence and athletic performance to the competing athletes. Paralympic athletes need to be subject to the same exacting standards and constructive criticism as their able-bodied counterparts. I think this is particularly true because athletics is an individual sport and you are competing for yourself and against yourself. Your performance is entirely your responsibility, unlike the team sports where the one can always dissipate responsibility throughout the team.

This is exactly what I miss about team sports and particularly rugby. It is a wonderfully unifying and rewarding sensation to win a match as a team. The camaraderie and the sense of collective endeavour and achievement are special. I no longer play rugby: I can't afford to risk an injury. I now play touch rugby with a group of friends, which involves far less physical contact and no hard tackles and is a more relaxed and amateur game.

Water polo is another sport I have always enjoyed, and it has the added advantage of being something I can do without prostheses, but the truth of it is that I perform better in short spurts — sprinting and anaerobic sports. My issue with water polo, and it is the same with swimming, cycling and marathon running, is that it is an endurance sport and constitutionally I am better designed for speed rather than endurance. I believe this is a question of muscle fibre and physical predisposition. Even when I was at the height of my physical fitness and training specifically for these sports, when I played water polo I always arrived at the last of the four sessions which comprised the match totally exhausted. My performance, whether it was in water polo or rugby, was about my explosive energy, energy which by definition was not consistent for the full length of the match.

Once a sportsman turns professional he or she is forced into making choices in order to excel at his or her chosen sport. From my perspective today, as an athlete and a sprinter, it would be counterproductive for me to cycle 20 kilometres. I am sure I am fit enough and one could argue that it would only further my general wellbeing and all-round sporting fitness, but as I do not want to encourage my body's development of slow-twitch muscle fibre I make sure that it does not have the opportunity. Slow-twitch muscle fibre is of course significant, because in athletics reaction times are everything. My commitment and focus on my career as a sprinting athlete mean that, however much I enjoy water polo and rugby (the latter a sport that keeps you running pretty much for the full eighty minutes of every match), I no longer partake in anything that is detrimental to my preparation and chances of success.

Even when I work out at the gym, two minutes is the maximum length of any one exercise, and even that is an exception. *Underground Secrets to Faster Running* by Barry Ross, who was a coach for more than thirty years, has revolutionised my approach to my physical fitness and training. He was one of the first to understand that it is vital that one's training reflect the nature of the sport in question — in other words, training sessions for sprinters need to be short and focused. Another example is the difference between pull-ups and push-ups. As in athletics you need to propel yourself away from the ground it is recommended that I train using push-ups, as that way I am pushing my body away from the ground, whereas pull-ups would require me to pull my weight towards something. Every detail of your training package must be designed around the result required. I concentrate on short explosive movements: for example, I will jump from a platform and as soon as I touch down immediately spring forward towards another, thus training my body to push away with ease and speed.

When I train I use my ordinary everyday prostheses, not my running blades, and early every morning I work out in the gym under the instruction of Sebastian Rothman, a celebrated former boxer and exceptional personal trainer.

Nutrition is another aspect of my life that has been transformed since I committed to my career as a professional sprinter. I no longer consume as many carbohydrates as I used to, since I have no need to build and maintain important energy reserves. In order to sprint effectively I need energy to burn quickly, and so it is logical that I need to eat large quantities of protein like chicken or fish. As a rugby man my favourite treat was to eat five slices of bread thickly coated in peanut butter, and I could get away with it as I was burning the calories during the match; sprinting, however, does not consume as much, and in any case one's body uses only the energy stored in one's muscles, so I have had to give up that particular pleasure.

Originally I had thought I could simply swap rugby for athletics and carry on as before, but it soon became clear that the choice was more complex. I studied the different types of muscle fibres and spoke to a number of people qualified in the field of sports science; it was quickly apparent that to be a successful sprinter I would have to give up rugby altogether, and I must confess that within three weeks of giving up rugby my qualifying times improved significantly. The same can be said of my nutrition. Although giving up carbohydrates meant that I was more tired by the end of a training session, I was and am far stronger and my muscles repair far more quickly. Obviously this knowledge has deepened as my experience in athletics has grown, and I have gradually adapted myself to the discipline.

To be a professional athlete is as much a lifestyle choice as it is a career choice and it requires sacrifices in every aspect of one's life. In what may seem a trivial example, it is not possible to be a professional athlete on only five or six hours' sleep a night. Training hard is not enough: one needs a minimum of eight or nine hours' rest, since it is imperative to train both body and mind. My life has changed enormously over the last four years. For example, on Saturday evenings when I could in theory go out as late as I want as I do not train on Sundays, I generally end up watching a DVD at home. By ten o'clock I can hardly keep my eyes open and even when I go to the cinema I often end up falling asleep in the middle of the film — embarrassing but true. Ten years from now I am sure my life will be different, but right now I have to be totally dedicated to what I am doing in order to do it properly and succeed.

Most of my friends in my peer group are

university students and are living and enjoying a lifestyle that is diametrically opposed to mine. They are out late at night socialising, drinking and going to parties. I believe that there is a time in life for everything, but for the last four years I have been engaged in other activities and my perception of life and of what is important has changed a great deal — inevitably, a gap has opened between us. Some people tell me that I am no longer the same person; to some extent they are right; I have seen and been exposed to many new things and my eyes have been opened to other life choices. It is a situation with which I feel very comfortable.

The anti-landmine project that I am now involved in is a good example of something that is now close to my heart and that has completely shifted my perspective on the world. I was as naive and as self-absorbed as the next man, but the opportunity to travel and actually witness what was going on changed this. I can no longer ignore that a mere 600 kilometres away from my home town, in Mozambique, so many people have lost and are continuing to lose limbs to landmines. In addition, many live in terrible poverty without basic comforts like a roof and running water. South Africa too has high levels of poverty and hardship (there is a township not 50 kilometres from my front door where life is very difficult indeed). I know that if I had not been blessed with fame and success I would never have become aware of these people's struggles. Today, because of my profile and celebrity, people ask for my help, they invite my involvement and show me where my participation will bring added value to the people and cause in question. As I have matured I have come to realise and value my own good fortune in life and, at the same time understand the humanity of others.

Today, my main goal in life, alongside my sporting goals, is to help others. I would like to build my own nongovernmental organisation to assist African amputees, both financially and otherwise, in obtaining prostheses. I would like to find a way to manufacture prostheses at a reduced cost. I know from my research along with my own personal experience that the cost involved in manufacturing the prostheses is not enormous in itself, but of course the manufacturers have to maintain a profit margin. If we were able to manufacture the prostheses directly, the savings involved would permit people — for the same outlay — to buy three pairs instead of two pairs at today's prices. I discussed my idea with one

Above: 'I had the dates of my mum's birth and death tattooed on my arm. It's the only tattoo that I have...'
© Stu Forster/Getty Images

Right: '13 July 2007, the day of the 400 metres at the Golden Gala in Rome, is a date that I will never forget...'
© Stu Forster/Getty Images

Above: 'Spectators in Sheffield welcomed me with the warmest applause...' © Michael Steele/Getty Images

Above: 30 April 2008, Lausanne
© Fabrice Coffrini/AFP/Getty Images

Above: 16 May 2008, Milan 'I was once again free
to compete! Peet and I exploded with a cheer...'
© Piera Bossi/AGF

Above: Beijing 2008; winning the men's 100m final
© Li Wen/Xinhua Press/Corbis

Above: Beijing 2008; winning gold for the men's 200m
final © AFP/Getty Images

Left: Beijing 2008; on the podium, after winning gold for the men's 100m
© AFP/Getty Images

Above: Beijing 2008; out of the starting blocks for the men's 400m final
© AFP/Getty Images

January 2008; in Manchester for the launch of the BT
Paralympic Games © Getty Images

Above: 1987, Dad, Mum and I on the day of my christening © Pistorius family archive

Above: Mum and I
© Pistorius family archive

Above: 'I remember that summer, at Plettenberg Bay, two children asked me why I left only holes in the sand, rather than footprints…'
© Pistorius family archive

Above: 'In March 1998 our little sister Aimée arrived'
© Pistorius family archive

Left: 28.10.1988, Plettenberg Bay
© Pistorius family archive

Below: 1989, with Carl and Mum
© Pistorius family archive

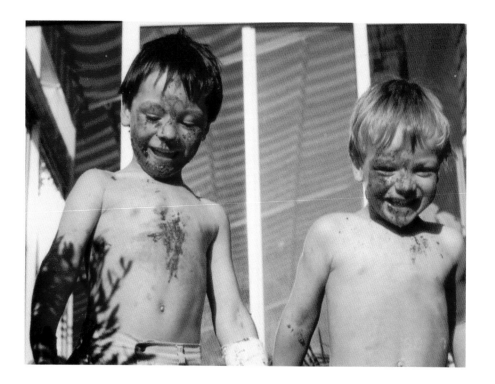

Above: 'Carl was my little tempter, capable of pushing me to my limits and then beyond, just like Buzz with Woody in *Toy Story*...'
© Pistorius family archive

Left: 'I loved the beach, the sun, those serene summer days...'
© Pistorius family archive

Above left: 'At seventeen months I had my first pair of prosthetics. They were very comfortable.'
© Pistorius family archive

Above and below: 'At the age of two I was a little pest with blond curly hair, long at the back and short on top and my Mickey Mouse shoes...'
© Pistorius family archive

Left: 1992. First day of school at Constantia Kloof Primary School
© Pistorius family archive

Above: November 2001. My mother's second marriage
© Pistorius family archive

Above: Party at Pretoria Boys High School with Aimée
© Pistorius family archive

Left: 'I worked very hard, under Ampie's guidance, with the aim of improving my times…'
© Max Rossi/Reuters

Below: 'I had to confront mythical figures of paralympic sport such as Marlon Shirley…'
September 2004, Athens
© Louisa Goulimaki/epa/Corbis

of the scientists who oversaw my tests during the appeal process before the Arbitration Tribunal in Lausanne — about which more later — and he explained to me that the technology necessary to produce low-cost, lightweight but resistant and therefore low-maintenance prostheses exists already. In an African context this is very important: we do not have the infrastructure necessary to provide long-term maintenance easily and affordably to all who need it, and furthermore, with the enormous distances involved a doctor will often fit prosthetic limbs but have no opportunity for follow-up clinics with the patients.

Today it is easy for me to use my name to help other people, and for precisely this reason I feel it is my responsibility to do as much as I can to make a difference. I think that many celebrities consider this a burden that they can address simply by donating money to charities. I would never wish to suggest that financial donations were not vital, but I feel strongly that it is important to be personally involved and to lend your time and support to initiatives you really believe in. There is so much need both here in South Africa and abroad.

On a personal level, I have chosen to get actively involved in helping people in

Mozambique. Mozambique was an obvious choice for me as a Southern African, as indeed was the subject of landmines given that I am an amputee. I found myself inspired, in a way that is comparable to my encounter with the incredible swimmer I met at the Athens Paralympics, by the manner in which people make do and succeed with what they have. Many of the Mozambicans I met had very little in the way of material comforts or money and had undergone trauma and hardship, yet instead of complaining about their lot they were getting on with life, doing their best and living happily. Their love of life and positive approach was contagious: it reminds me to value my life and to remember how lucky I have been. I find it immensely rewarding to help these people because they delight in what life is giving them. I struggle far more when people call me in desperation asking me to help one of their loved ones who has lost a limb, perhaps in an accident, but who is mired in anger and depression and refusing to get out of bed and learn to walk with prostheses. It is tough for everyone involved, but it is almost impossible to help someone who does not want to be helped. Often I find myself telling these people stories of those I have met in Mozambique, in the hope that I can inspire them and help them understand their good fortune even when it has been tainted by the experience of an accident and an amputation. A seventy-year-old Mozambican woman particularly moved me. When we gave her a pair of prostheses she had not walked in thirty years. That same day she learnt to walk again and by the end of it was moving around without the help of others. Sometimes perspective is all that is required for a person to understand that despite undergoing an amputation they are nonetheless alive and well and able to make the most of the incredible advancements that medical science and technology have to offer. Unlike many people who find themselves in similar circumstances but do not have enough money to put food on the table, let alone buy a pair of prostheses, regaining something approaching their accustomed quality of life will be easy for them. Everything, of course, depends on your attitude to life. You have a choice: take what has happened to you as a slight from destiny and the theft of your natural right to have two legs, or simply embrace life and relish the new opportunities and knowledge that will come with the change.

If God were to ask me if I wanted my legs back, I would really have to think carefully about my answer. I do not feel remotely as if

I have been short-changed by life. Had I been born with normal legs I would not be the man I am today. My less than ordinary life has helped my potential shine through. I am not sure that I would have had the same motivation and determination to improve myself and become an athlete. People often ask me what it is like to have artificial limbs but I am unable to answer that question. My prostheses *are* my legs, I have never known others and so I invert their question and ask them to explain to me how it feels to have legs. There are downsides to having prostheses: for example, should I sit down to a meal with a beautiful woman and she started playing footsie with me under the table I would be at a real loss! This remark may sound flippant, but behind it is a serious point — the inestimable importance of embracing life's vicissitudes with good humour. One should try to celebrate, or at least enjoy, what one cannot change.

In my experience, there is little that a sense of humour cannot remedy. I always make fun of my legs. Recently an older gentleman asked me if I regularly went out partying with my friends. I was rather perplexed as I could not see the point of the question, but I nevertheless told him that if I was not training the following day then yes, I did, probably once every two months or so. Not satisfied, the gentleman asked me if I was a heavy drinker? No, I answered. With a broad smile on his face, he then told me that he understood that as I was already legless there was no need for me to be a heavy drinker. I found the remark hilarious — what I particularly appreciated was that he accorded me the same respect and treatment as he did all the other people present. I hate being the recipient of people's pity and am insulted when people adjust their behaviour on my account. Being legless is not in itself particularly funny, but this does not preclude the desire, indeed the need, to approach it with humour. There is a saying that I hold dear that goes as follows: It is not our disabilities that make us disabled but our abilities that make us able.

We all have limitations, be they mental or physical, of varying importance, but at the same time we are all equipped with so many more capacities that make it possible for us to transcend disability. People often ask me how it is that with artificial legs I can be qualified as anything but disabled. My answer is that, being far more able than they are in more than 90 per cent of sports, why should I be qualified as a disabled sportsman? It has been said that using prostheses is proof of disability, but I fail to see why this aspect of my persona should overshadow all my sporting ability.

One project that I support is called Sole of Africa, an NGO that was founded by Richard Branson to help landmine victims in Mozambique. Another is called the Chaeli Campaign and was born from the concern and initiative of five nine-year-old girls. One of the girls was born with cerebral palsy and degenerative neuropathy and she needed an electric wheelchair, but her parents were unable to afford the expense. The girls banded together and started to make chocolate slabs, which they then sold. Within two weeks they had raised 20,000 rand (about £1,800 at the time), which was more than enough to cover the cost of a wheelchair. But still the girls kept on going, donating their gains to various charity organisations. Today they are between thirteen and fifteen years old and they have started their own NGO, which has financed the acquisition of over 170 electric wheelchairs for needy South African children and an equally significant number of pulleys to help lift paralysed people into or out of their beds, baths and so on. It is a wonderful example of people getting together to help one another.

Recently the Chaeli Campaign started a

soup kitchen in Cape Town staffed entirely by people with mental disability. There is no menu; one eats whatever has been cooked that day, and they do not accept payment, only donations. The kitchen employs people who would otherwise struggle to find work and also provides a forum for people to talk and support one another — and, not least of all, keep out of the way of trouble. The money received is divided among the staff, with any leftovers going to different charities. It is a fantastic project that has given people back their self-respect and independence, and it also educates the wider community that there is another way to integrate people into society and provide them with genuine support. The restaurant has become quite popular within business circles.

There is a project which I am very keen to kick-start — it will be very expensive but worthwhile in the long run. I would like to have a truck redesigned to contain a fully equipped laboratory able to travel throughout Africa and help people where they live and work. Basically we would need to be able to arrive in the village in the morning, see the patients and supply them with durable and affordable prostheses that same day. There are already numerous organisations trying to clear the land of mines but very few which specifically take care of those who have already lost limbs.

I learnt so much from the people I met in Mozambique. The experience has changed my life and made me into a better human being. My only regret is not being able to share the experience with my mother. I am sure that she would have heartily approved of my attempts to help those less fortunate than myself in this moment of triumph and fame in my life. It has certainly been a privilege for me. She always felt that things happened for a reason and that giving one's time and support was the only way to unite and overcome adversity. I like to think that she is proud of this part of my life as she watches over me.

8
Golden Boy

I have been blessed with an unusually rich and rewarding life for one so young. Alongside my growth as a sportsman, I have also experienced the joy of being involved in a very strong and committed relationship. Vicky was my true love and the power of our relationship bolstered me immensely. Our relationship was very intense and, although this most probably contributed to our eventual separation, it meant that while we were together we approached every moment as though it was our most important, indeed our last. We had a very fiery relationship and often rowed. One summer stands out for me and demonstrates the folly of reacting too quickly. It was December 2005 and I had decided to join some of my friends who were holidaying in Durban, approximately 650 kilometres from Johannesburg. Vicky was in Johannesburg but we spoke to one another often. One evening after an exceptionally nasty argument I decided that it was imperative that I immediately return to Johannesburg and make peace. Ignoring my better judgement, I left Durban at 3 a.m. About halfway into the journey exhaustion set in. I should have pulled over and slept a bit but instead I continued and of course nodded off at the wheel. I woke up as my car ploughed into the guardrail; one side of the vehicle was completely destroyed. I had a really lucky escape but the car was a write-off. My behaviour was unforgivably stupid and I regret it to this day.

For all the fire, Vicky and I were very happy together. On Valentine's Day in 2006 Vicky awoke to find that, while everybody was sleeping, I had been to her house to hang two hundred coloured balloons (I blew each one up individually!) in the trees, in her driveway and on her fence and then once that was accomplished I took a can of spray paint and artfully wrote 'I Love You, Tiger' on the road in front of her front gate. That morning she awoke convinced that I had forgotten Valentine's Day only to open her front door and discover my tribute to her. She was deeply touched and phoned to thank me with tears of joy.

In April 2005 a dear friend of mine, Ryan, was involved in a terrible motor accident and after a week in hospital passed away. I was devastated and went through a period where I was so sad and depressed that I simply withdrew into myself. Vicky took my behaviour as a rejection of her, and I was unable to communicate anything different. Somehow we lost the ability to share with one another. In May I decided to head to England for two weeks and take part in the Disabled World Cup in Manchester, but my real reason for going was that I wanted to avoid dealing with the barrier between Vicky and me. It was while I was in Manchester that we finally split up. It was awful, and the fact that I was abroad made it even more painful. On my return home I tried to talk to her and sort things out but it was too late. Vicky felt that I had alienated and rejected her and was unmoved by my protestations to the contrary. We were actually both incredibly angry and did not speak to each other at all for the next eight months. It was one of the lowest points of my life.

Despite the turmoil of my personal life, my career continued to progress in leaps and bounds. I was training intensively and seeing the fruit of my efforts. During 2004, in addition to having competed in the Athens Paralympics, I had also run in a number of different races (100, 200 and 400 metres) recognised by the International Association of

Athletics Federations (IAAF). Then in March of 2005 I competed in the 400 metres at the South African National Championships and came sixth. Thanks to this result I began to receive invitations to important events in the international athletics calendar — for example, the Helsinki Grand Prix which takes place in August every year. I was not able to make the journey to Helsinki that year, but the mere fact of being invited represented an important success and a new level of recognition for me.

Sadly, my success did little for my morale. I was most unhappy and cried at the drop of a hat. In short, I missed Vicky terribly. Her absence left a gaping hole in my life as she had been both my girlfriend and best friend — the person with whom I shared everything. I missed her intelligent advice, her conversation and of course her physical presence. I was preparing myself to move out of my Uncle Arnold's house (I had lived with him and his family since my last year at school and we remain very close) into my own home, and as Vicky had been instrumental in choosing both the house and the furnishings life seemed rather cruel to me.

My relationship with my father was also subject to some new stresses and strains. When I started out in professional athletics my father had taken on the role of managing my career, and this change in the dynamic between us exacerbated an already complex bond. After all, I was only eighteen, and this change in our relationship coincided with a new-found need to rebel and gain some independence and freedom for myself. It was a steep learning curve for both of us, and eventually we came to the joint realisation that although work is very important, family is far more important. My finding a professional manager gave each of us a second chance. My father has since moved to Cape Town where he has a new partner and is managing a sulphate mine, a job from which he derives great satisfaction . . .

In 2007 (after having had three managers, including my father) I signed up with Peet van Zyl. It is a truism to say that for a totally committed athlete who is training intensively and travelling frequently, a manager is a quasi-father figure. By definition you spend a lot of time together, and that person is involved in both the professional and more personal aspects of your life. I remember my brother Carl being particularly resentful when I chose to spend my holidays with my manager; it did not help that Carl did not like him, but I think people on the outside do not always grasp how close this relationship can be.

Peet is a marvellous manager. He is very selective in choosing the athletes he represents, which is ideal as it means he is more able to focus on each of us individually. He is a calm, level-headed and positive presence in my life and always seems to manage to sort out the fixes I get myself into. On one occasion I called him in a flat panic. I had lost my legs — my blades, to be more precise. I was packing my suitcase as we were departing later that day for America and I had turned the house (and my car) upside down but was still without my blades. Fortunately Peet had a spare pair at his office so calamity was avoided, and it turned out that a friend had played a prank on me by hiding my blades, blissfully unaware that I was about to fly off for a competitive race.

I wish I had had Peet at my side when I ended up behind bars. It was the end of August 2006. I had been working out at a shooting range with a friend of mine, and as it had been a very physical exercise I am assuming that some of the gunpowder must have rubbed onto my prosthetic limbs. One week later I set off for Assen in Holland as they were hosting the Disabled World Championships. Initially I had planned to fly in and then out immediately after the competition, but I needed to spend a week in Iceland working with the technicians and design team at Ossur who produce my Cheetahs, so at the last minute I decided to change my ticket, fly to Iceland from Amsterdam and then back to South Africa via Amsterdam. Before leaving Johannesburg International Airport I went to the counter to have a new ticket issued, but as their information systems were down they issued the ticket manually, promising that they would update my new journey details onto the system as soon as possible. So far so good; I headed off to Assen and triumphed, winning a gold medal and improving the world record in all three of my chosen distances. Then on the return journey between Reykjavik and Amsterdam I somehow managed to lose my ticket. In Amsterdam I went directly to the check-in and explained what had happened to the staff there. They struggled to believe me, as when they checked their computer system my name was missing from the list of passengers. They told me they were unable to help me and sent me to the airport police to draw up a claim for the loss of my ticket, adding that I should then return to them with my claim in hand. This I duly did, but the staff shift had since changed and the flight attendant in charge feigned total incomprehension at my explanation. Within five minutes I found myself flanked by two police officers who asked me to follow them. When I asked for some clarification they abruptly told me not to try any smart tricks and that I was accused of having made a false declaration as I had never been in possession of any ticket to Johannesburg. I could not believe the absurdity of my situation and all my tales of my original ticket having been manually altered fell on deaf ears. They did tell me that they would look into the situation but that I would have to wait for the outcome behind bars. After three hours in the company of a decidedly fishy-looking cellmate a police officer arrived and without much fanfare told me I was free to go. I was delighted, and as it was about fifty minutes before my original flight was due to take off for Johannesburg I set off at a run, bags and all, towards the boarding gate.

I had almost made the flight; all that remained was to pass through the security check. My prostheses often cause problems at security checkpoints as they tend to set off the metal detectors, and this time was no different. I explained to the police officer that

I was an amputee and made use of prosthetic limbs and, as had been my previous experience, he then asked me to follow him into the cubicle where he would be able to examine me and my prostheses more carefully. I had started rolling up my jeans so he could examine my prostheses when he explained that it was normal procedure for them to check my prostheses by examining them with an explosive-sensitive device. It was a novel experience for me but I took his word for it and did not think much of it when he left the cubicle with his device in hand and the polite explanation that he would be back in a minute. As I sat daydreaming four police officers burst into the cubicle and, screaming at me, told me to turn with my face to the wall and my hands behind my back, as I was now under arrest. It looked like a scene straight out of a cop thriller, and I was dressed for the role with a black bomber jacket, black cap and impenetrable dark glasses. They promptly and abruptly returned me to the police station where I had been held earlier in the day, but this time I was treated with a whole different type of respect, to the point that my previous cellmate was now visibly intimidated by my presence and would not even look me in the eye. It was as though the police officers had been validated in suspecting me of criminal behaviour and nefarious intentions.

It took them another twenty minutes to explain to me that my prostheses had tested positive for explosive substances. I was absolutely flabbergasted. Now I was being accused not only of falsifying a ticket but, far more seriously, of terrorism! I was horrified and panic-stricken, and yet my situation seemed so absurd that I felt like I should be laughing. A police officer explained in the tersest manner that they would need to carry out further tests on my prostheses and so left me handcuffed in the cell to sit it out. By that point I had well and truly missed my flight and my personal belongings and cell phone had been impounded. I spent the next two hours worrying and wishing that I had had some way to forewarn my Aunt Diane that I would not be arriving in Johannesburg the following morning. Then, again without warning, an officer appeared with my belongings in tow, and told me that I was free to go as the security risk had been neutralised. Miraculously I managed to find another flight leaving Amsterdam for Johannesburg and have never been so relieved to take off and return home.

I must confess that what most bothered me during the whole surreal experience was the fact that my cell phone battery was dead. I was so used to having my mobile by me, and so reliant on being able to communicate at any time, that I felt completely isolated. My inability to phone and forewarn Aunt Diane and also to share what was happening to me with Vicky weighed heavily on me. At the beginning of 2006 Vicky had enrolled at the University of Cape Town, and, although initially it had been very difficult and painful for us both, we had started spending time with one another again. We both missed one another and so it was a bittersweet relief for each of us to begin to rebuild a friendship.

At that time I was training hard under Ampie's tutelage with the objective of improving my speed in order to qualify for the Beijing Olympics in 2008. All the indicators were that this was an entirely achievable goal, as I was in perfect physical condition and running very well. But then, as my qualifying times continued to improve, I was surprised to notice that they brought with them a far greater critical interest in my performance. People within the athletics world started to imply that my 'high tech' legs were somehow giving me an unfair advantage and needed to be handled with suspicion and more circumspection. I was unprepared for this, as my carbon fibre prostheses have been on the market for over ten years now and are commonly used by amputee athletes. Suddenly my struggle to qualify for the Olympics had been transformed into something far more fundamental — it became a contest about my very right to run and participate in the Olympics.

As I have mentioned, I had been invited to compete at the Helsinki Grand Prix in 2005 but had been unable to attend. At that point my qualifying times simply were not good enough to compete at such a high level. But by 2007 my qualifying times had improved to the extent that I had come second in the 400 metres at the South African National Championships, and I now felt the time was right to compete internationally. Coincidence would have it that this was also the moment that the International Association of Athletics Federations (IAAF) adopted a rule which would make my participation impossible.

The IAAF met in March 2007 in Mombasa, Kenya, and ruled to modify what is known as Rule 144-2 (I can now recite it off by heart). Basically it prohibits the use during a race of 'any technical devices designed to improve performance'. It expressly prohibits the use of 'any technical device that guarantees to the athlete making use of this technology an advantage over those athletes not beneficiaries of this technology'.

Many knowledgeable sports commentators speculated that possibly the rule had been brought into existence to prevent me from competing in able-bodied international athletics competitions, not only because of its wording and implications but because of the expedited manner in which the decision was passed. For example, Track Fast, who are behind various British sporting events, and who had invited me to compete in Glasgow, immediately contacted me to explain that on the basis of this IAAF decision they felt obliged to cancel my invitation. Interestingly, though, I had not received any official notification from the IAAF and ostensibly the ruling had nothing to do with me.

In June of that year the IAAF issued a press release which stated that article 144-2 was not to be interpreted as concerning my sporting participation, at least not until sufficient testing could prove that my prostheses were in fact a 'technical advantage' over my fellow competing athletes. Nick Davies, the IAAF press secretary, telephoned Peet and clearly stated that as things stood there was no interdiction to my participation and I was free to compete. There is no doubt that all the polemic, along with the confusion that reigned, made the situation difficult for me. I did my best to keep my head down and focus on my training, and I was absolutely overjoyed when Peet contacted me to tell me that I was registered to compete in an important race in Rome.

Peet had been in contact with Gigi D'Onofrio (a man for whom I have great respect) who is the organiser of the Golden Gala event in Rome and who was quite happy to accept any criticism or negative press interest that my participation was likely to attract. It was hugely important for us to have established such a good relationship with this intelligent and open-minded man, who was happy to take responsibility for his choices. He gave me the opportunity to prove myself on the world stage.

And so it was, after two years' preparation, that in July 2007 I set off for Rome. I was so excited by my good fortune and the marvellous opportunity that lay before me.

The date 13 July 2007 will be engraved in my memory for ever; it was the day of the 400-metre race. The weather was magnificent, and we took the bus to the stadium to warm up and prepare for the race. The setting was striking: the stadium is a spectacular edifice surrounded by ancient statues of Roman athletes. The public support was strong and the atmosphere in the stadium electric. That evening the race was taking place at the Olympic Stadium. As the build-up to the race picked up momentum I was particularly nervous. I was used to competing in South Africa against athletes who were all familiar to me and from whom I more or less knew what to expect. This, on the other hand, was an entirely new and intimidating challenge. I had to force myself to focus on giving my best and making the most of the occasion.

I started the race quite slowly but, as is my style, picked up speed and by the last hundred metres I had moved from seventh position to finish second in the race. I was exhausted but jubilant. I had come second with a time of 46.90, but more importantly it was the first time ever that a differently abled athlete had competed alongside able-bodied athletes at international level.

9
Swimming against the Tide

With the golden gala behind me, I left for England the next day where I had been invited to compete in the Norwich Union British Grand Prix in Sheffield, which is an equally prestigious competition.

This is more or less where the similarities stop. The atmosphere in England was completely different. The press seemed to be leading the controversy that surrounded my participation by giving exaggerated column space both to unsupported insinuations as well as a more technical debate about the supposed advantage represented by my prostheses. They were soliciting public participation by launching opinion polls on my case. It was very difficult for me and left me feeling insecure.

The sports reporters chose the pre-race press conference to bombard me with questions regarding the IAAF ruling. I did my best to keep my calm and reiterate a point that I considered of paramount importance, namely that had I believed that my Cheetahs provided any sort of technical advantage over the other athletes I would have retired from the competition myself. I valued the principles of fair competition and good sportsmanship above all others. Of course, my thoughts (and my answers to their questions for that matter) held little sway with the press corps who continued hammering on.

Admittedly my morale was low, but the final straw came when I awoke on the morning of 15 July, which was the day of the 400-metre race. It was raining heavily and of course no athlete likes to compete in those circumstances, but for me it is particularly disastrous, as my Cheetahs don't perform exceptionally well on a wet track.

As race time neared the weather showed no sign of improving and so I found myself facing a difficult decision. Was it preferable to pull out of the race and miss the opportunity to compete (an opportunity that, considering the prevailing furore over my invitation to the event, now seemed even more valuable) or race, however nasty the climatic conditions, and risk a disappointing performance that would be both embarrassing in the press and perhaps prejudicial to my goal of qualifying for the Olympics. I had never before backed down in the face of a challenge, but on this occasion for the first time I seriously contemplated it.

I was incredibly stressed and struggled to concentrate during the warm-up. The downpour continued unabated and the rubber track was very slippery; what was more, I was running alongside the invincible Jeremy Warner who at that time was the fastest man in the world over 400 metres. The only light on the horizon was the warm welcome given to me by the Sheffield home crowd as my name was announced over the loudspeakers.

The race began and within the first 100 metres I could feel I was losing pace. Try as I might, and I gave the race my all, I did not manage to pick up any speed, and I crossed the finish line last. Then to add insult to injury I was disqualified from the race for having left my lane. As I said, no athlete likes to run in the rain — it is not pleasant, and you can barely see where you are going with the rain in your eyes. But with my prostheses I have an additional problem, which stems from the fact that my knee joint is further away from the ground. The higher your knee joint the more interference there is with the way in which you perceive the point at which your foot touches the ground. To have a good push-off, good balance and control it is imperative you train in the same climatic conditions so that you become used to the experience.

When I look back, and taking the climatic conditions into account, I did not run a bad race that day. My time (47.65) was closer to my personal best comparatively speaking than that of any of the other competitors, and I was particularly disadvantaged by the rain. So even though I came last and the result was hardly flattering for me, I was competing against the best and the fastest in the world. I am proud of my performance in Sheffield and consider it a personal victory, because I compete first and foremost against myself but also because competing alone that evening was a mighty challenge.

Again, at the press conference after the race the journalists took me to task about my performance. The general thrust of their questioning amounted to why it was that I insisted on being able to compete against able-bodied athletes. Why should I be permitted to compete in able-bodied athletics when the Paralympics are designed precisely for people like me? Again and again I explained that I had no objection to competing in the Paralympics, but saw no reason why, if my talent and ability permitted me to run within the qualifying times which were prerequisites for the various able-bodied sporting events, I should not be permitted to do both.

The upside of the controversy was that I received support from the majority of athletes and many of the organisers behind the top events in the international sporting calendar, and this has been immensely valuable to me. I think they appreciate that the qualifying times that I have achieved demand significant sacrifice, effort and training — equal to the sacrifice, effort and training undertaken by able-bodied athletes — and that for this reason I am not a 'disabled athlete' but just an athlete.

The exemplary athlete and holder of the world record (19.72) in the 200 metres discipline for over twenty years, Pietro Mannea, has been very vocal in his support of me. He has publicly stated that in his professional opinion (and with his experience on the track) the controversy surrounding my blades is nothing but absurd, since it is undeniable that running without the perception of one's feet on the track — whether the track is dry or wet — will have a significant technical and psychological impact with consequent knock-on effects. What is more, athletes of his stature train for many hours

145

every day in the run-up to important races, whereas I am obliged to curtail the time I spend training as the prolonged and intense chafing of my stumps against my prostheses often leads to the development of sores and injuries. In Pietro's words, if one takes these two aspects of my physical and mental preparation into account, along with the intense training and sacrifice necessary for me to achieve this level of competitive performance, one can only commend me as an example of pure athletics. I have often wished the IAAF saw in my participation the same paradigm.

There are of course some athletes who see things differently. Marlon Shirley, the world-famous Paralympian athlete and 100-metre champion (he ran the 100 metres in 11.08), commented a couple of years ago that as he is a single amputee (officially classified as T44) he does not believe it fair that he should have to compete against a bilateral amputee (T43) like myself. He took issue with the fact that during the Athens Paralympics I competed against the T44 athletes but, as I have stated, I made this choice precisely because there were no T43 athletes with qualifying times anywhere close to mine.

With the Sheffield race behind me, I returned to South Africa, feeling very dispirited. The atmosphere in England, fuelled by all the negativity and controversy in the British press (aided and abetted by the British downpour), had thrown a pall over my achievement and I had come seriously to doubt that I would receive a second chance as the IAAF seemed absolutely set on ruling against my prostheses. Even the South African media, who had always been among my staunchest supporters, had begun to doubt my actual athletic talent.

The sporting season was over but I knew that the coming autumn would bring with it the greatest of all challenges. The IAAF had decided to take the necessary steps to put the controversy to bed; they had scheduled tests for November 2007 to prove definitively whether or not my prostheses constituted a technical advantage over other athletes. The tests were to be held under the aegis of the Cologne Sports University and to be supervised by the renowned Professor of Biomechanics, Doctor Paul Brüggemann, in conjunction with Mr Elio Locatelli, who is responsible with the IAAF for all technical issues.

In actual fact the IAAF investigation was already under way: the IAAF had decided to make the most of my participation at the Golden Gala in Rome to install high-resolution cameras right along the length of the track, so as to provide themselves with the technical footage necessary to analyse whether or not my prostheses could in fact be considered a technical advantage over my competitors. I had been advised that there would be additional cameras concentrating on the race but I had not been informed that the purpose of these cameras was in fact to document each moment of my race and in turn measure my stride. Only much later did it become public knowledge that Mr Locatelli considered my Cheetahs responsible for artificially allowing me a wider step.

After studying the recording of the race in detail the technicians at the University of Rome came to the conclusion that my stride was not longer than that of other athletes. They did note that in comparison to other athletes my performance followed a different phase development. Unlike most able-bodied athletes, who reach the apex of their performance within the first 70 metres, I start the race slowly but then pick up speed, peaking between the 200- and 300-metre marks. This conclusion then spurred Mr Locatelli on to request that I be subject to further testing.

The tests were scheduled to take place in Germany on 12 and 13 November 2007 and were structured in such a way that my performance would be analysed and measured alongside five other able-bodied athletes who had run the 400 metres with qualifying times similar to my own.

I felt confident that these tests would definitively prove my position and show once and for all that my prostheses did not in any way afford me a technical advantage over other athletes. I hoped that by persuading my critics I would also be able to clear my way to realise my dream and participate in the Olympics.

The tests themselves were conducted in a circus-like atmosphere. I was at the centre of a throng made up of doctors, scientists, technicians and then the cameramen who were filming the procedure for the IAAF; the pressure on me was intense. My only support was Peet, my manager, who did his best to lift my morale, but it was a challenging experience for both of us, further complicated by the knee injury I was nursing at the time.

This was the first time ever that the IAAF (or anyone else for that matter) had dedicated time and resources to researching the question of prosthetics. The use of prosthetics was completely unregulated, particularly when compared to the reams of regulations that apply to the type and design of the running shoes one can use while racing. The reason for this was because until I was admitted to compete in the top-tier competitive athletic events, prostheses were only used in Paralympic events. In actual fact there is very little to differentiate between the prostheses on the market today (basically they are designed according to the weight of the person who will wear them). This is partly because there are so few companies that produce prosthetic limbs (namely the German companies Isatec and Otto Bock and the Icelandic firm Ossur, which has been supplying me since 2004). I feel strong in the knowledge that this is not simply a debate about my athletics and my dream to compete in the Olympics, but rather that it is about discrimination — for me any athlete who shows sufficient talent and dedication should be allowed to take his or her place and compete against the best in the world.

Once the tests were over I left Germany feeling relaxed and optimistic. Unfortunately it did not last for long. In December 2007 the IAAF sent me their official report, which stated that over a distance of 400 metres my prosthetic limbs did indeed constitute an unfair advantage over other athletes. This amounted to a banning order, which would make it impossible for me to compete among able-bodied athletes internationally. Professor

Brüggemann concluded his argument by explaining that, in his opinion, carbon fibre prostheses constitute a 'mechanical advantage' when one analyses the energy restored to the athlete by the blade (the bottom of the prostheses). The scientists had compared the movement in my prostheses with what happens to the human ankle when maximum sprinting speed is attained and had concluded that at that moment I was benefiting from an unfair advantage over the other athletes.

In synthesis Professor Brüggemann's report states the following:

- I am able to run at the same speed as able-bodied athletes while expending 25 per cent less energy because once I attain the speed in question, running on prostheses requires less energy outlay than running on normal limbs.
- The mechanics of racing while running on prostheses is totally different from that seen among able-bodied athletes, as is the energy restored from the track to the athlete. The energy restored to the prosthetic limb is over three times higher because it has a flexibility quota of over 90 per cent, unlike that of a human foot that is unlikely to exceed 60 per cent.
- A prosthetic limb loses about 9.3 per cent

of the energy unlike the human ankle that loses more than 41.4 per cent and so in other words the mechanic advantage given by the prosthetic limb can be quantified as more than 30 per cent.

Basically my prostheses allow me to run at the same speed as other athletes while expending far less energy, and it is for this reason that I am at my best towards the end of the 400-metre race and not at the beginning.

The experience was traumatic for me on many different fronts. To begin with, I was disappointed with the way the publication of the report was handled by the IAAF. Before I was officially informed, the report was leaked and published by *Die Welt* on 19 December. I learnt about the report's final conclusion and my consequent exclusion from international able-bodied competitions from the newspapers. It was a devastating blow. Initially I clung to the hope that it was an incorrectly reported journalistic scoop, but the truth was of course confirmed when the IAAF finally delivered my copy of the report to me a few days later. I was distraught at the conclusion of the report.

As the saying goes, it never rains but it pours. In December 2007 Vicky and I finally separated permanently.

After our initial break-up we had got back together in June 2007, but it was never plain sailing. I trained and travelled intensely and she was living in Cape Town. We tried to see one another on alternate weekends with one of us always flying to spend time with the other. In addition I did not approve of her new group of university friends, and this caused much friction between us. The difficulty of maintaining a long-distance relationship weighed heavily on us, and so in early December 2007 Vicky decided to move back to Pretoria. We spent the holidays with my siblings but then on New Year's Eve we had a terrible argument that proved fatal to the relationship.

We have not spoken to one another since, but I care about her and respect her deeply. I wish things were different because she is an incredible individual and I have always imagined sharing my life with her.

10

The Finishing Line

The year 2008 got off to a rough start. My break-up with Vicky left me emotionally raw, and then the IAAF had given us only until 10 January to comment on the Brüggemann report.

Peet and I discussed the findings with experts from all over the world, but in particular with Professor Robert Gailey of Miami University. Everybody seemed to agree in principle with the statistical findings that had emerged from Professor Brüggemann's research but not with his interpretation and use of this data. In addition we thought it important not to be discouraged by, and therefore appeal against, a decision that took only the advantages of prosthetic limbs into account but considered none of the disadvantages. Professor Gailey did not contest the validity of Brüggemann's data but postulated that for it to be useful and truly reflective of my performance it was essential that each phase of the 400-metre race be analysed in the same manner. Any analysis that examined only to the final phase of the race was by definition limited and therefore incorrect when applied to the race as a whole. In addition he argued that it was vital to take both the positive and negative consequences of prosthetic limbs into consideration. It was one thing to study the advantages the Cheetahs provide over normal ankles/feet but one must also consider the differences in my physical development as a whole. Furthermore, the IAAF ban prohibited me from competing at any distance — 100 metres, 200 metres or 400 metres — whereas the Brüggemann report stated that my supposed technical advantage over other athletes could only be demonstrated in the last 200 metres of a 400-metre race.

Professor Gailey and my other supporters pressed me at the very least to request the IAAF to allow me a period of time in which I could attempt to bring my prosthetic limbs into line with their standards, as is typically the case during the approval process for able-bodied athletes' shoes.

Throughout this process Professor Brüggemann clearly stated that his brief was in no way concerned with the ethical, political or social implications of my competing but had only been to verify the scientific/technical

156

advantages (and not even the disadvantages) afforded by my prosthetic limbs, and that in addition his research had always been specifically limited to the final phase of the race. The position of the IAAF was rather more ambiguous: Mr Locatelli, the Chief Technical Officer for the IAAF, is on record explaining that their reservations were also geared towards the future of the sport, and making sure that one day there were not people with wings competing on the track.

Professor Brüggemann's report indicates that the locomotion, the actual dynamic of movement while sprinting, while wearing this type of prosthetic limb, is completely different from that required from a normal human body while sprinting; the dynamic is entirely different. And, further, that from a purely technical point of view, in the context of high-speed sprinting, this specific type of prosthetic limb certainly carries an advantage at the ankle joint level; however, it is probable that the prostheses in question concurrently incur disadvantages for the hip and knee joints.

On 10 January 2008 we replied that in our opinion the tests performed in Cologne were both biased and limited in scope, and that therefore we rejected their conclusions.

On 11 January the President of the IAAF,

Mr Lamine Diack, wrote to each member of the IAAF Executive Council reiterating that the tests had confirmed the thesis of a 'technical advantage'. The members then had to vote, with the result being to ratify the ban to prohibit the use of prosthetics such as mine. Unfortunately, this outcome meant that I was promptly and officially banned from participating in able-bodied athletic competitions.

The IAAF left no avenue open to dialogue, and we had no choice but to appeal against their decision before the Court of Arbitration for Sport (CAS) in Lausanne, Switzerland, and ask the court to re-examine my case. It was a difficult time for me and I was feeling very low, but I decided to focus on maintaining a positive attitude and doing all I could to prepare myself for the second round of tests.

We needed to compile a team of influential and authoritative scientists who would be able to run the tests and also command respect internationally. Through a friend I was able to contact Professor Hugh Herr at the world-renowned Massachusetts Institute of Technology (MIT) and Professor Roger Kram from the University of Colorado; they were joined by Professor Peter Weyand from the Rice University in Houston.

Dewey & LeBoeuf, a well-known international law firm with an impressive reputation in the sporting world, had also contacted me. They felt so strongly about the merits of my case that of their own accord they offered their help. I was astounded at how quickly they managed to collate all the information necessary and relevant to my case.

The next step was to fix a time when all three scientists and their respective teams would be available to meet and work together. As I had agreed to be present at the awards ceremony organised for the Laureus Awards in St Petersburg in Russia on 18 February, we agreed that I would fly directly from Russia to Houston and begin ten days of intensive testing.

From my perspective, Houston was an entirely different experience. First of all, before each test the team took the time to explain to me exactly what was about to take place and to what purpose. It was rather like a crash course in bioengineering, and I learnt a lot from it. The scientist in charge of the testing had decided to begin by repeating exactly the same tests performed by Professor Brüggemann and his team, so that we would have something to compare against. In addition, they suggested I undergo VO2 tests (the testing which is considered the best indicator of cardio-respiratory endurance and a reliable predictor of athletic performance, demonstrating the measured maximum amount of oxygen consumption by the muscles at peak rate with the least effort) on a treadmill and not a bicycle, so that the conditions simulated would be closer to those of a foot race. It was soon clear that the Houston results would differ from those charted in Cologne.

This was a huge relief to me, as the IAAF had relied heavily on these specific test results to demonstrate my technical advantage. Over a period of ten days I participated in many different tests; at times I thought that I was repeating the same experiment endlessly, but in reality there were slight but significant variations both in the focus and in what was required of me. My acceleration was studied in detail; my oxygen consumption was measured at different speeds at different points during the race, as was the conduct and handling of my individual prostheses. I learnt much over this period, and left Houston feeling resolved and confident that the process would prove that the tests in Cologne had been inconclusive. Too many variables had been excluded for the tests to be considered the basis for a ground-breaking decision which would change the face of international sport for ever and result in my being banned from able-bodied competitions. I felt that the process and the results of the testing in Houston would set the record straight on my account but, more importantly, would also be a step forward for the standards of athletic competition internationally.

I had not been back in South Africa long when I was asked to return to Houston to undergo further examination. I obliged and promptly flew back for another eight days of intensive testing. By the end of March we had reached the definitive conclusion that in no way could my prostheses be considered as giving me a technical advantage over other athletes. When one considers all the hard work and emotional turmoil, all the controversy and speculation, it was immensely gratifying finally to be able to repudiate my critics and show that my achievements were mine alone and dependent on my commitment, training and talent and not my prosthetic limbs.

Still, with the tests behind me, the battle was not yet won. We had to wait until 30 April, the day on which the Court of Arbitration in Sport had convened a hearing and to which all the concerned parties had been summoned.

I soldiered through this difficult time by

keeping my mind focused on my training schedule and with a little help from my new home and a new and special presence in my life.

At the beginning of 2008, I had started going out with Jenna, a delightful, sweet-natured, beautiful girl with blonde hair and sparkling blue eyes. She was eighteen. We had been honest with one another from the outset and I had explained to her that I was still not entirely ready for another serious relationship. On some level I still missed Vicky terribly, and although our relationship was over I still had to come to terms with the hurt I felt. I was of the opinion that it was important not to rush into things, and I feel that we have a beautiful relationship because we took the time to get to know one another, and because our relationship developed from a strong and meaningful friendship.

My new home in Silverwoods, one of the nicest and greenest parts of Pretoria, has gone a long way towards helping me feel more stable and rooted in my life. After my mother's passing and my years in boarding school I found that I was yearning for a space of my own that I could make my home. In truth the house is much larger than I need, but I wanted it to be somewhere I would be able to grow into and where all of my family and friends would be welcome to spend time or just drop in. Everybody who knows me knows that no formal invitation is necessary. I had a carpenter make up a wonderful and very substantial wooden table which is my pride and joy, as I can think of nothing better than reuniting all the people I care about around a large table and some good food. I am still very close to my brother Carl and have told my sister Aimée that she is welcome to come and live with me. The house is open-plan and all on one floor with wide doors so everyone — the old, the young, as well as those among my friends who use wheelchairs — is at ease and feels comfortable moving about. It has a number of television screens so we can all hang out together and watch sport, along with a fantastic sound system and a great barbecue area so we can make the most of being together and celebrate life. I have not forgotten the harder times of my youth and feel so lucky today that I can share my good fortune with my loved ones.

One day I would love to buy a Ferrari or a Lamborghini. I adore sports cars, but that is for the future. A house is something you can share with all those you care about whereas a car is more about personal gratification.

When the time came to travel to Lausanne

163

to the joint International Olympic Committee and the Court of Arbitration in Sport headquarters, I was a heady mixture of nervous anticipation and dread. Fortunately Peet was at my side throughout. The hearings took place over two days and, although I found the pace intense, I was absolutely gripped.

President Martin Hunter working alongside the judges David Rivkin and Jean-Philippe Rochat composed the judicial team. They set the tone by pointedly reminding all concerned that I had not been accused of any wrongdoing; their mandate was only to examine the issue objectively and study the data and conclusions of the two different tests to come to a well-considered and factually correct decision as to whether my prosthetic limbs could indeed be considered as a technical advantage of any sort. As the judges did not have the benefit of a court-appointed technical expert they asked all the experts present, German and American, to come together and take the time to explain to them the technical aspects of the question pending, along with the rationale behind and process followed for the different tests and, of course, the conclusions reached. It was rather unusual to see everybody come together and debate and dissect the matter intelligently and dispassionately, without the adversarial climate that is often created when you have two opposing teams and a person in the dock who has allegedly committed some misdemeanour.

I found the experience absolutely fascinating. I had not really understood until then the revolutionary nature of the testing programme. It really was the first time that a bilateral amputee athlete had been deemed capable of competing at such a high level, and so there was no data or parameters against which to compare the information gathered during my tests. In addition, as I had been tested twice, over two intense periods of time and close together, the tests provided more of a snapshot of my capability at that point in time than any definitive conclusion. The only other athlete who is also a bilateral amputee and competes at a similar level is an American university student who is in any case an Iron Man triathlon champion and specialises in long-distance swimming, cycling and running. Our sporting styles are hardly comparable.

The tone of the court hearings was not relentlessly serious. At one point the President found himself wondering out loud how one would analyse the movement of a kangaroo from a bioengineering perspective. No sooner was the thought out of his mouth than Professor Roger Kram from Houston jumped out of his seat excitedly explaining that he was in fact an expert on the movement of kangaroos and that he had even tested them by having them jump on a treadmill equivalent.

I also found the hearings psychologically very demanding. Not only was this my last chance, but my battle, which had started as a personal quest born out of personal frustration, had developed into a symbolic fight against discrimination. I felt that I had come to represent all people like me, both today and in the future, who play sport or anything else for that matter and who want to be treated as equals.

My lawyers share my point of view. In fact they initially contacted me and offered their services to me free of charge after being struck by the inherent contradiction in the IAAF's position on my case. The IAAF has an ethical code of conduct, which it adopted along with an international code of conduct concerning disabled people, and which enshrines and protects an established 'right to normalcy' for all. My lawyers (based between the USA, Switzerland, Italy and South Africa) had been following my case and immediately saw an opportunity to explore this problem and hopefully make a contribution that would be important in the development of civil rights more widely.

I was in Italy when the Court for Arbitration in Sport finally passed judgement. I think I have a special relationship and love for Italy because I have enjoyed two of my sweetest victories while there. The Golden Gala was a unique moment that marked my life, and then, of course, there was the day that I learnt the conclusion of the CAS. The fact that my Uncle Leo has shown that our family originates from Pistoia simply makes the attachment stronger for me.

I was in Milan on 16 May 2008, waiting in the offices of my legal firm. We had been informed that the court was expected to make a pronouncement that morning, so we gathered to share the tension and give one another some moral support. I was unspeakably anxious, feeling nauseous from the nerves, dejected and exhausted. To kill time I decided to go shopping, but I was unable to concentrate and undecided about everything so we headed back to the hotel. We were standing in the hotel lobby chatting when I noticed Marco, one of the Italian lawyers, moving away from the group. I thought little of it at first but then I noticed him coming towards me attentively reading the page that he was carrying in his hand. As he came closer to me he seemed to be consumed by emotion but I was still not sure whether this was elation because the decision had found in our favour or dejection because he was going to have to explain to me that the decision had gone against me. Under normal circumstances Marco is a phlegmatic chap, and the care he was taking to read slowly was apparent to all.

Eventually Marco turned to me and explained that the court had ruled that on the basis of the data collected it was not possible to conclude that my prosthetic limbs (and the judgement refers to my actual prosthetic limbs as opposed to prostheses in general) gave me a technical advantage over the other athletes, because at no time was it conclusively proven that the advantages of competing with prosthetic limbs outweighed the immense disadvantages of competing with those same prosthetic limbs. The court ruled that the ban against me was null and void and I was free to compete again. It was a surreal moment for me and it took a while for the significance of the decision to sink in. It was everything that I had hoped for and yet the reality of it still swept me away. We were all jumping up and down, shouting in delight and hugging one another.

The press conference had been scheduled for three o'clock that afternoon, and as the CAS had been firm in requesting a press embargo until that time we had to be very careful to keep the news private. This was not as easy as it may seem: we arrived at the press conference half an hour early and it took all my self-control not to break into a broad smile and crack jokes with the full house of journalists. At three o'clock on the dot, Peet rose to his feet and said: 'The Court of Arbitration in Sport has decided as follows . . . ' Then he broke into a wide smile. The applause was fantastic as the room exploded in cheers and the noise of cameras clicking and flashes snapping. It was a unique moment, overwhelming and unforgettable. I was ecstatic and very proud. Amazingly, by the time I turned on my cell phone after the conference I had 160 congratulatory messages and numerous missed calls.

Finally the controversy and the insidious gossip were laid to rest. The IAAF released a statement to the press in which Lamine Diack expressed his delight at the outcome of the appeal process. This was all immensely gratifying for me; as I had said in my statement before the CAS, my life has not always been easy but I have had the good fortune to have enjoyed a normal and healthy

169

relationship with able-bodied people, both in the sporting world and elsewhere, and at no time have I felt 'disabled' or different in the way I had been made to feel when I had been banned from participating in competitions.

Now I was free to think about my future. It was time to get back to what is most important for me: running. My dream is to be the fastest man in South Africa and, with time and a lot of hard work, perhaps even the fastest man in the world, with or without legs.

In my opinion, one of the most important legacies of the CAS decision is to state clearly that the excellent qualifying times and the many achievements of athletes like myself, amputees who run with prostheses, are entirely their own achievements based on merit and talent and not, as had been implied, due to the quality of the prostheses. And furthermore, these athletes display not just incredible talent but also immense tenacity as they have each overcome the disadvantage of having to run with prostheses in the first place. The judgement was pronounced by the most authoritative body regulating the sporting world: there is no other body to appeal to, and this fact, along with the content of the decision, will set a precedent for any future cases. I hope that it will serve to inspire people — sportsmen and

— women, disabled and abled — to commit themselves and work hard in the confidence that they can achieve the highest rewards and believe in the power of sport.

I always like to quote Pietro Mannea's words: 'Sport is like an elevator, everybody should be allowed to ride in it.' I feel strongly that sport must be a unifying force in society, bringing all elements, colours, religions and sexes together, and that this can only be meaningful if it extends to uniting able-bodied and disabled people. Having grown up in South Africa with its recent past of racial discrimination and violence I can't emphasise enough how important this is to me. To know that my struggle may just help other people today or in the years to come makes a big difference to me.

11

Beijing

No sooner had the drama of the CAS drawn to its happy conclusion than the Beijing Paralympics beckoned.

In truth, the work for Beijing had started several months earlier because of the extra training I had put in to try to qualify for the Olympic Games. What this meant was that I was more than equipped for the 400 metres, but the 100 metres and 200 metres were a completely different story. Therefore, as soon as I returned after my qualification attempts for the Olympics, the 100 metres became my sole focus for the next two months.

The 100 metres is by far the most demanding event for me at the Paralympics. There are some really strong contenders, and I knew that if my start wasn't up to scratch my goal of three gold medals would wither away. Ampie, my coach, along with Sebastian and Vincent, my body conditioners and gym trainers, needed to make me powerful and lean. Giving them the task of achieving that within a two-month period was some demand. But I was lucky, as everyone around me understood the time and sacrifices I needed to make in order to be ready for the world stage.

The day had come for me to pack for the Games and already there was a huge expectation that I would deliver. The team met up at the airport in Johannesburg and for the first time in months I was back in uniform. After twenty-seven hours of flights and transfers we arrived at the Paralympic Village. It was eleven o'clock at night yet it was humid, verging on uncomfortable. I remember everyone including myself being frustrated and tired. We were ready for bed more than anything, but as my head hit the pillow my mind wandered off to the challenges ahead. The next morning I woke up in my little white room and looked out of the window for a view of the village. My roommate, Arnu Fourie, an amputee sprinter, a great friend and one of the greatest examples of a gentleman I know, was also staring out at our new temporary home; neither of us could remember much about the village from the night before. It wasn't long before we were dressed and showered and ready to indulge our inquisitive minds, so off we embarked on an exploration of the village.

It was extraordinary! The dinning room was about 200 metres by 100 metres and the gardens were amazing. There was also a huge selection of arcade games and internet points located around the village to keep the athletes' nerves from eating away at their confidence.

The one thing that I particularly enjoyed was that every night at eight o'clock they had a cultural show in a small amphitheatre that offered a particularly agreeable way to unwind and reflect upon the next couple of weeks' targets. The smallest details were taken into account at the venues, including a religious centre in the village where, I must confess, I found it hard to contain my laughter while listening to the Chinese priest trying to deliver the service in English on Sundays.

The day before the opening ceremony Ossur — the leading company in sports prosthetics — decided to host a press conference for its athletes. This included some of the top Paralympic sprinters of all time. I caught a cab and arrived at the venue in downtown Beijing a little late. I guess I wasn't ready for what was to happen next, but it certainly gave me an intense surge of adrenalin. I walked straight into a waiting room, which was about 5 metres by 5 metres, full of all my strongest competitors, one of whom was Marlon Shirley. I hadn't seen him for four years as he had pulled out of every competition as soon as I entered. He had beaten me in Athens in the only 100-metre sprint we have ever run against each other, but since then I had broken his world record every year.

Awkward doesn't even come close to describing how it felt. Sprinting probably involves more elaborate mind games than any other sport. Of course, everybody acted as if they were completely relaxed, but as soon as the programme coordinator came to call us you could feel the tension as everyone made for the door. We took our places at the front of a room jam-packed with international sports journalists and media companies. Needless to say it didn't take long before each athlete was playing their game and forecasting the race. When it came to Marlon he stupidly claimed that the 100 metres would be his as he hadn't lost a race in eight years. I managed to suppress a grin. I knew that Marlon had just given me the fuel to show him that the track belonged to me.

Athletics is brutal. I went last and the press asked me what I thought, to which I answered: 'The 100 metres is going to be one of the greatest races of the Games, be sure not to miss it!' I decided to keep my ammunition for the track; I knew that there I would get my point across more than clearly.

The 100 metres is the most nerve-racking of all three races. I only run a handful of them every year, and tend to focus on the 400 metres. What this meant was that if I managed to win the 100 metres, I would feel far more confident in the 200 metres and 400 metres. My start and first thirty metres are not as good as those of the single amputees, and therefore I knew that I would have to perform at my peak to take the 100 metres.

The semi-final went well. I ran an 11.16-second race, and this placed me first, which was about right as athletes usually run 0.3–0.4 seconds slower than in the final. I was really looking forward to the final, but there was to be a greater plan for the race. I woke up on the morning of the big race and looked outside; it was overcast and windy. The weather report confirmed my fears of afternoon rain. My race was at 4 p.m. and when I got to the track it was pouring. My spirit was unsettled but Ampie talked me back into the right mindset. Seeing Marlon and Brian Frasure out on the warm-up track made me want to run like I had never run before.

An hour before the race we gathered in the final calling room where all the athletes have to meet about forty-five minutes before a race. Once again, the tension was high — uncomfortably high. At this point you wouldn't want to be anywhere else, but at the same moment you wish you were holed up in a log cabin listening to classical music in front of a roaring fire — and yet everyone looks supremely relaxed. I reckon any sprinter could win an Oscar for their acting skills in that waiting room.

As we walked out onto the track this feeling merely intensified, but by now I actually did see red and wanted to rip the track up. Marlon and Brian weren't my only worries, however. Just as I had come from nowhere in 2004, this time there was another athlete to watch out for: Jerome Singleton, a talented sprinter and one of the most humble yet deserving athletes I have ever run against. Jerome had amazed everyone in the semi-final, in which he finished second behind me, with a really quick time. In all honesty he had no need of mind games and attitude: he was more intimidating than any other athlete as he had proved himself where it mattered, on the track the day before.

We lined up, Marlon on my left and Jerome on my right. I knew that they would both fly out of the blocks, and that I had to stay with them and not let them pull more than 2 metres ahead of me. The time had come, and down we settled in the blocks as the rain dripped from my brow and trickled into my mouth as my breathing intensified. I placed my fingers firmly on the wet Mondo track just behind the white line as the crowd of eighty thousand plus people hushed. At this moment I knew that I would have to cut my driving phase (the first 30 metres) shorter as the track was wet and I was worried about slipping to around the 20-metre mark — in effect coming upright more quickly and pulling the ground beneath me instead of pushing it. I prayed to God for the power and glory to be His and closed my eyes and waited.

At this point the 100 metres becomes the most surreal of experiences. Everything seems to slow down until you can feel your heart beat, yet the rate at which you can process thoughts is phenomenal. Once you cross the finish line your recollection of what has happened in the previous ten to eleven seconds is close to minimal. As we went on the set position I inhaled and waited . . . waited . . . wai . . .

BANG

First thought, movement of alternate arm

and leg, second thought, stride placement for first complete stride. The next couple of thoughts were either misaligned or I simply wasn't thinking at all. By the time I got to the 10-metre mark I was nearly upright, and as I watched the field run away from me I had to make a serious analysis of my current position and motion. By the 30-metre mark I was about 5 metres behind Jerome, who had an overall lead of about 2 metres. He had made one of the most phenomenally quick starts I've seen in a long time. I had some serious work to do, and I can't tell you how the next 40 metres unfolded, but as I saw later in video replays, I reached the fastest speed I have ever managed in my life.

There was one particular stride around the 90-metre mark that gave me the couple of extra centimetres I needed at the end. I dipped Jerome on the line and wasn't sure who had won. Jerome ran up behind me as we looked up at the time board and as my name came up first he exclaimed, 'Where did he come from?' He had run an amazing race and as I turned around to congratulate my competitors I saw Marlon lying on the line. He looked as if he was in pain and I later heard he had twisted his ankle.

I went up to him and extended a hand to help him up; either his pain or his ego got the better of him as he refused it. This, however, was my moment, and I believe the top three fully deserved the result. I was ecstatic. I ran up to Ampie who was shaking his sixty-year-old bones like a teenager. I had missed the gold in the 100 metres in Athens but I had made sure that this one was mine. In the commentary of the race the shouting as I crossed the line was, 'You wouldn't have bet a dollar on him at the 50-metre mark but you would've made a million at the end!' That was good enough for me . . .

Going into the 200 metres and 400 metres was a lot easier. My confidence went up and I was beginning to acclimatise. The 200 metres is my favourite event as speed is still crucial, but the start has less influence on the race as a whole. The day of the 200-metre final came and I wasn't feeling great. My chest was tight and my head was thumping lightly. Nevertheless, I was really excited to be running the race. My goal for the Games was three gold medals and at least one world record. I had missed the world record in the 100 metres but I realised I had been lucky just to win the race; but the 200 metres, my next race, was up for grabs. The stadium was near its capacity of ninety thousand people. The cheers were awesome. As I walked onto the track I was shaking my head. Arnu looked at me and said, 'I know, isn't it just amazing?' The aura, the emotion, the sheer excitement was going to make this race a big one.

I ran the race with all I had, getting off to a far better start than in the 100 metres, and at last I was running on a dry track in the Bird's Nest. This track was FAST — a relatively hard surface, with the Mondo laid in such a way that its elasticity was enhanced, making for exceptionally quick times.

The 200 metres wasn't going to give me the time I needed for a world record, yet I was happy with the race. Standing on the podium and listening to the South African national anthem for the second time allowed me a moment of reflection on the year. It was a bittersweet reflection, but for the year to be ending on such a high note was more than I could have expected.

By the time the 400 metres came I had picked up a nasty chest infection and found myself tired and frustrated. I had started to compete on the second day of the Games, and now, nearly two weeks later, I was ready to bring the whole experience to a grand conclusion. Staying focused for that long really deserves a medal in itself!

I woke that morning to find that it was

raining again. As I went down to breakfast Ampie handed me a paper which informed me that my race had been moved to the last athletic event of the Games. The closing event at the Bird's Nest: the final moment of truth. My physical state remained poor for the rest of the day and by the time I left for the track I was in a terrible mood. I arrived at the warm-up track in the drizzle and sat under the grandstands watching for about an hour, every now and then glimpsing an athlete as visibility was now down to about 30 metres. I thought about the Games, the job at hand, my tired muscles, but most of all I thought about my goal for the Games: three gold medals, one world record. The 400 metres was my strongest race. Could I do it? I didn't have an option: as long as I was capable, I would do it. I didn't want to look back one day and regret not using my talent to the full.

I walked out onto that track, in the rain. I did my thing. I ran a hard race but more than anything I ran a clever race. As I crossed the line I felt like death but looked up at the board. There next to my name were the two letters I longed for: WR.

For a brief moment I was in a state of pure ecstasy; I was at peace with my performance. During my third time on the podium I felt very alone. The podium was huge, and I realised I had not achieved all this on my own. My coach, trainer, body conditioner, physio, chiropractor, dietician, doctor, manager, family and friends deserved to be up there with me. They too had dedicated time and effort, made sacrifices and commitments in order to put me centre stage. I wished they could have been alongside me in that moment of glory.

They are always in my thoughts, and I will never forget their role in helping me to achieve my highest goals. In my life I have always tried to make the best of a situation, look for the positive and go forward with a smile. I feel that it was my destiny to be born as I am, and that my experiences and my life story as a double amputee have made me who I am today. But this journey has not been undertaken alone.

Most of all, I think of my mother. I know that she is watching over me, and although she died before I began sprinting and was not alive to witness my success or my gold medals, I know that she takes great pride in me. I consider myself fortunate to have had such a special and wonderful mother and shared the happy times we had together; just thinking about my mother gives me courage and peace of mind.

There is one thing that is very special to me

indeed. It is the recording that my mother made during a radio interview about me that was aired in 1999 when I was fourteen years old. I listen to it so often that I can recite practically all of it off by heart, and it never fails to give me that warm fuzzy feeling and make me smile.

'Oscar is a dynamic and sporting child; he is even-natured with a delightful, bubbly sense of humour. He loves to joke around and laugh and is always positive. I hope that my words can give hope and encouragement to those listeners who have also experienced trauma and suffering.'

It is my wish that my mother's message of hope should live on in this book.

Letter One:
Carl Pistorius to Oscar Pistorius, Pretoria, 4 May 2008

Dear Oscar,

As a family we have always shared everything. Our parents led by example and always included us in their discussions, however delicate, and you and I have been close confidants for as long as each of us can remember. Even so, there are a few things that I have held back, within myself, perhaps because of a gauche sense of modesty mixed with prudishness, perhaps because until now the time has not been right, or there has simply not been enough time to say them properly. Here goes, let me tell you about yourself from the beginning, as I remember it. I hope my letter will bring a smile to your heart and be useful for your biography.

When I sit back and watch the family films that I store in my memory, I treasure a particular image of our mother holding you in her arms. I think you must be about nine months old and I am three. I see us clearly; in fact I think this is my first conscious memory of our life.

I remember our mother on the first floor of our Johannesburg house as she tells me about your feet. I was tiny but it was the first time that I understood that there was something different

189

about you. Mum let me touch your feet, gently of course, and stroke your toes. You still had feet and toes then. I realised then that your feet were unlike mine, and that you were special. Everything about you was special to me.

It is astounding how transparent this memory is for me. Mum and I are sitting side by side on the sofa and she is holding you in her arms. Gently she lifts the blanket that is covering you and lets me hold your little feet. I don't think that she explained in great detail what was different about your feet, nor that you were going to have an operation, but in her subtle style she made me aware of your presence and your needs. I have never really thought about it until now, but I think I can say that it was the first moment in which you became part of my life, up until then you had only existed on the periphery.

I remember our mother walking up the stairs with you in her arms, while I was climbing alongside her on her right. I was still so small that I had to climb up each stair and could not be said to walk up them! I think she had friends round for tea.

You see, Oz, my first memory of myself is also my first memory of you.

My next memory is your first pair of prostheses. They were carbon fibre tubes with a flat bottom but without feet that were supposed to alleviate the build-up of pressure on the bone.

You learnt to walk with those prostheses. I can remember Mum putting your prostheses on in your bedroom in our Johannesburg house and then bringing you through to the corridor where you would practise walking down the passage. It is incredible to me how crystal clear this memory of you is, you must have been about one and a half and I would have been four. After a while I was allowed to help you put the prostheses on. I remember Mum carefully explaining to me how to attach them and where I had to remove the Velcro strap so as to remove the pressure from the stump. She showed me where the bone had been amputated and how it forms a sort of a bump. I remember being very curious about that bump and desperately wanting to understand why it formed where it did and how it had happened.

These are beautiful memories for me, full of tenderness and affection because that is how it was when we were small. To begin with we fussed over you but pretty quickly you lost your position on that special pedestal and had to get on with things by yourself. And that was pretty much when we started to really play together.

In the beginning we were bicycle mad. I used to attach your little blue and white plastic bicycle with a rope to my saddle and then tow you around behind me, up and down the stairs,

inside, outside, regardless. I taught you everything I knew! We also enjoyed playing with cars
and you were often willing to swap your newer
cars against my more trashed vehicles, all I had
to do was convince you that mine were in fact
better which was really very easy as you put
blind faith in whatever it was that came out of
my mouth! Those were the days. Only joking!
You wised up to my tricks very quickly.

Oz, I think you are a remarkably trusting guy,
and you are never judgemental, you are very
open-minded and intelligent in your approach to
understanding the situations life has thrown at
you. Sometimes I think people misinterpret you
because you are friendly, kind and polite to a
fault with everyone. But of course, as you know,
and I know, there is a huge difference between
sharing experiences and information and really
opening yourself up to someone and allowing
them to become part of the very small circle of
people that you trust absolutely. In fact I think
you are a far more reserved person than the initial
impression you give people.

I think it is also a legacy of our childhood. Dad
has always taught us to be friendly with all but
to need no one, to be strong and self-sufficient.
He was quite a disciplinarian and often told us
that he was not interested in spoilt or rude children, we could be naughty and mischievous but
we had to take care we never stepped over the

mark. It was always a mark of honour for both of us to impress our father.

In fact Dad was very strict with us, particularly before the divorce. Whenever we came to him in tears and looking for reassurance after having got into some fix, he would reprimand us and tell us that crying was only for weaklings and sissies. He hated our whining and made a point of teaching us to solve our own problems and clean up after ourselves the hard way. He was a loving father but also a hard man who expected the best from us and whose standards were always very high. He always spurred us on, pushed us forward to be courageous, to try new things, to want to improve ourselves. He brought us up to believe that we could achieve whatever it was that we wanted to achieve.

Do you remember that go-kart my godfather made for me? It was without brakes and we used to literally fly down the hill leading up to our house, in fact we used your prostheses to come to a halt and burnt through countless soles on your shoes in the process. By the time we finally came to a halt, your blind terror at our speed would have reduced you to a gibbering wreck but you were always immediately ready to walk back up and start all over again.

And do you remember that time we decided to climb up that brick wall, pretending to be rock climbers, but attached with a hosepipe. I remember asking you if the hosepipe was safe and resisting the strain, you answering yes and then of course the hosepipe snapped and I fell the four or so metres down to the ground. I broke my arm, but you were the one who was crying and distraught. I think you felt terribly guilty and so in the end I was the one that consoled you.

Then came the age of rollerblades. You were good at blading, much better than I was. You spent all your time blading, in fact to this day I remain convinced that it is the rollerblading that was instrumental in developing the muscles that you now use to run. I remember how compli-cated it was for you to get them on and off again as rollerblades have a reinforced ankle section but as you don't have an ankle there was no joint to flex to help your foot in and then out. A night-mare. You were a wonderful blader who invented some incredible tricks. In particular I remember you picking up speed and then leaping forward and landing dramatically onto your knees and then sliding forward like a music/film star. Once you realised that the fibreglass that protected your knees also prevented you from hurting your-self, there was no stopping you. You were fearless.

When you were growing up your legs were replaced often but never often enough, as you

were so active and rough on your legs the prostheses suffered a lot of wear and tear. Every
three months or so we would have to go back
to the technicians to have the fibreglass readjusted because inevitably you would splinter
or actually break it. In addition Mum used to
take your clothes to a special tailor to have
your trousers reinforced with particularly resistant patches so that you would not hole them
quite so easily. If she did not do this you
would tear your trousers within an hour of
having put them on. This all required preparation and time and so on those occasions that
you required a more elegant wardrobe Mum
had to plan in advance. I remember going to a
wedding with you, Mum had given you a
brand new pair of trousers but you ruined
them pretty much immediately as you were
climbing all the trees, sliding and then falling
out of them, not to mention the friction
caused by the fibreglass and the prostheses
rubbing against the fabric.

Whenever possible we could be found climbing up whatever was available. In my opinion this
was how you developed your incredible sense of
balance. And do you remember how heavy your
first prostheses were? I think it must have been
unbelievably onerous for such a small child to
carry such a heavy dead weight all the time; it
was like a permanent workout for you. You wore

those prostheses until you turned twelve or thirteen and as you grew older so your limbs became bigger and heavier too, which explains how you came to develop your athlete's butt.

At the time we slept in a bunk bed and every night we fought as to which of us was going to sleep on top. I remember Dad obliging us to take turns. We hardly ever used the ladder; the test was to put our hands on the side and to use the strength in our torso muscles, shoulders and arms to pull ourselves up onto the top bed. You were really strong. I remember you sitting on the kitchen floor and then pulling yourself up onto the counter with the strength in your upper body alone. It was around this time that Dad made your prostheses two rather oddly shaped artificial socks made of sheepskin; the idea was to protect your limbs as the fibreglass tended to crack when it became too cold.

Our Honeydew house was fantastic, paradise for children like us, there was no end of space for us to cycle in, or trees for us to climb. We were very lucky to have a father who worked very hard to provide for us materially (and who made the Honeydew house possible) and a mother who took such loving care of us. Admittedly it was only the first part of our lives but then again people do say that the early years are the most important ones. You and I were allies.

Of course with time things change. The age

difference that separates us, one year and eight months, is now irrelevant but as a child, and particularly in the period following our parents' divorce, I felt and took my responsibilities as the eldest child and the older sibling very seriously. I felt very protective towards you and Aimée but also of our family equilibrium. It was important to me that you and Aimée got on well and did not bicker.

Do you remember that I was awarded a scholarship, which I then refused as I was worried about leaving you and Aimée alone? When I started boarding school I worried incessantly that I would not be there for you should you need it and I was relieved when it was your turn to come to boarding school. Your starting boarding school coincided with Mum becoming engaged and I was happy and more relaxed as I believed things were finally settling down and there would be more space for me to let loose and express myself.

But then suddenly the bottom fell out of our world. It was 2002; our mother had remarried in November of that year and it was our first Christmas without our parents in the company of our school friends and grandparents. It had been a brilliant summer even though I had managed to catch hepatitis and had been very ill indeed. When Mum returned from her holidays she told me she had not been at all well over the month of December and it seemed that her symptoms were the same I had suffered before being diagnosed with hepatitis. My having had hepatitis convinced her doctors that she had hepatitis and so two further weeks went by with her being tested for hepatitis on three separate occasions. During this period she continued taking her medication, but unfortunately it was only later that we discovered that she had developed an allergy to it. Her condition kept worsening but I comforted her and told her that I too had been terribly unwell with hepatitis and that she would improve. By the time her doctors realised what was wrong and had her admitted to the hospital it was too late.

It was an awful time in our lives but doubly hard for me. For a long time afterwards I was racked with guilt, I have relived time and time again our long conversations with me sitting at her bedside and her telling me how unwell she was feeling, and my comforting her that it had been exactly the same for me during my illness with hepatitis. On one occasion she even asked me if I was certain that our symptoms were identical but I simply reassured her.

To this day I believe that my brush with hepatitis gave her a false sense of security and meant that she was not nearly attentive enough to her symptoms or to pressuring her doctors into finding both the necessary answers and a more appropriate treatment plan more quickly. Deep down I know that if I had not been ill with hepatitis her illness would have seen a different outcome. Having said that, I have come to accept that such is life, her illness is no one's fault only part of her and our tragic destiny. But it has been very hard for me and the fact that I have never really spoken about my feelings compounded it for me. I suppose I had to make peace with myself first.

I think now that the weight of responsibility on my shoulders and the role that I had carved out for myself as the eldest child after our parents' divorce greatly contributed to my behaviour. My first year in boarding school had been the first in which I had truly let my hair down and I had partied and drunk and smoked as much as possible without giving half a thought to the possible consequences. My wild excess was how I developed hepatitis and in retrospect I can't help but think if I had behaved differently things would have gone differently. I suppose when you are young, and I was still very young, you desperately need a reason to explain why things happen as they do. I was so close to our mother and her loss was an enormous blow and loss to me.

The sensation that I had somehow sacrificed my life and myself in vain when our mother died tore me apart.

You and I dealt with that period of our lives very differently. I mutated from being a polite, responsible, well-organised, studious and sporting young man into a wild rebel. I was out of control; I drank at school, regularly got into fist fights and partied all the time. Nothing held any sway over me. Nothing seemed to matter to me. Although I did not see things quite as clearly at the time, it was my way of coping with my grief and remains a period of my life in which I did a lot of growing up and learnt a lot. Your reaction was almost the opposite; you became incredibly focused and driven within your chosen sports and your training programme picked up in intensity.

After Mum passed away I did not want to return to boarding school, I wanted nothing to do with that world nor did I want to see anyone, whereas your initial reaction was to return to school and seek refuge among your friends. I remember how astounded and affronted I was that you wanted to return to boarding school on the evening of her funeral. I don't think I ever told you that your behaviour was beyond my comprehension.

Over the years our grandmother has played a vital role in keeping us close. She is an incredible woman and I love her with all my heart almost as much as I loved our mother. Throughout our lives she has been constant, she has stood by us and been the person capable of convincing each of us to listen to the other one and so have a greater understanding of opinions and approaches different from our own, and this time was no different. I think of her as the matriarch at the head of our family.

We struggled to see eye to eye during that time but fortunately our grandmother brought us back together. There was resentment and misunderstanding between us. I was consumed by my distress and sorting myself was more difficult than I could have imagined, and it seemed to me that you had deserted me in my moment of need. I felt that you were confiding in and being supported by your friends and had moved away from me. I know that you, Aimée and I are rather reserved personalities and that each of us is very cautious when it comes to emotions and the people to whom we entrust those emotions and, of course, that there is a big difference between friends and acquaintances, but the bottom line was that I felt alone and so it was that with time our mother's death became a taboo subject about which we talked little and infrequently.

Aimée's life was very different from our own and required different adjustments from her. While we were in boarding school she was living with our Aunt Diane but we spoke to each other often and spent weekends together.

I believe that our personalities and our lives

have been shaped by this experience. Part and parcel of our family's approach to life is the lesson that if you lose your way in life, no one can find it for you, you have to do it yourself. Only you can help yourself. You must rely on yourself to find your way and to stay true to that way. To be honest it took me quite a while to find my way again.

After our mother's death I was very caught up in myself, on the one hand I wanted and needed my brother and yet on the other I rejected everything, nothing touched me, nothing interested me. Our mother was no longer with us and as a result my life had lost its meaning, yet you seemed at peace with yourself and happy in boarding school surrounded by your friends. Sport, and your training, had taken over from your previous hobbies like passing the afternoon on the back of your motorbike.

After a while, once I had exhausted my alternatives, I too returned to boarding school. It was a good compromise; I decided if boarding school worked for you, it could work for me.

At least Pretoria Boys' High had your presence going for it and although I was not wild about your friends, and I had even managed to incur the wrath of the school principal, I eventually carved a place out for myself.

I can't say that I was much support to you over that time. Of course when I was at a low ebb, or you were, we would come and confide in the other one but that apart, we fought bitterly. We were both floundering our way through a hellish time of our lives.

Thank God that things are different today. Although we rarely speak of the loss of our mother and how much we miss her, we are very close again. It is difficult to know where to begin, we have such respect for one another and we are both discreet individuals. Fortunately for each of us, Aimée has been an incredible support to both of us. She handled our mother's passing better than we did and is a good listener. Our situation was different; you and I are so similar and it is terrifically difficult to see someone you love suffer terribly for the same reason that is causing you to suffer, it was so frustrating and left me feeling disempowered, there was nothing I could do, no way I could make it better. I felt so hopeless and struggled to simply let go and let time do what was necessary.

Even today we tend to share the good things in your life: your adventures, the wonderful and new discoveries you make on your travels around the globe, your new house, your dogs, women . . . The internet is more forthcoming than you are with information regarding your career. I know that we are joined by a bond that is far deeper than these novelties in your or my life and that if something important happened to you, you would share it with me and likewise. On a couple of occasions I have found myself sitting at home watching television while you are abroad and I have watched you on television. It is incredible; I get so excited that I am moved to tears, tears of joy of course. The last time I started shouting to all that would listen to me that you are my brother! I am so proud of you.

There have been other occasions where I have seen you just back from a trip and absolutely exhausted but unable to pull back, sit still and simply rest yourself. Although I respect your choices, I worry about you because you are my brother and I care about you.

Other people see you as Oscar Pistorius, the star athlete who has achieved the impossible, whereas I see you as a great athlete, but first and foremost as my brother.

People tend to think your life is all glory and celebrity but I know how hard you train and how much you sacrifice to make your achievements reality. Do you remember the last time, it was 11.15 in the evening and I had just landed after a flight back from Cape Town (there are only two cell phone numbers whose calls I will always pick up — you and Aimée) when you called in a state of anxiety to let off steam as the stress of the training programme, not to mention the awful wait for the court to pronounce its judgement, was taking its toll. I came straight to see you and

I will always be there for you in the same way as I know you will be for me.

A couple of days ago I was chatting with a friend. He asked me about you and I told him in no uncertain terms, 'I would give my left nut for my brother.' He laughed and told me that although I probably would it was unlikely that you would do the same for me. Well, I know he was wrong, I know that you would go the extra mile for me, and frankly even if I did not have this certainty it would not alter anything for me. This is not about a quid pro quo. Some relationships in life are based on unconditional love, and ours is one of them.

Carl

Letter Two:
Henk Pistorius to
Oscar Pistorius,
Cape Town, 6 June 2008

Dear Oscar,

My dear boy, recently I have been watching you on the television. You have made me so happy and proud that I can only wish that you too will experience similar joy when the time comes for you to become a father.

As you tell your story in this biography, I am honoured and delighted to be able to participate by sharing my memories, in fact it gives me the opportunity to relive parts of my life.

Before Carl was even born, your mother and I had decided that we would have three children. I had wanted a large family similar to my own, but your mother had laughed me out the room, nervous at the prospect of having to birth and raise a rugby team. Three seemed like a pretty good compromise to us both. If there had been only two of you there would have been no one to break the cycle of bickering, whereas when there are three siblings you can't argue with both simultaneously so you always have an ally and a healthy equilibrium in the family. Had I been able to choose I would have asked for our first child to be a boy and so I was elated when Carl was born. When our turn came to have our second child, Sheila asked the person performing her prenatal ultrasound to tell her the sex of her child so she knew you were on your way. I wanted it to be a surprise and so she kept the information close to her heart. When the time finally came and Sheila went into labour, her obstetrician asked me which sex I would prefer. I replied that the child's sex was unimportant to me; all I wanted was a healthy baby with ten fingers and ten toes. That would be more than enough. How ironic destiny can seem.

When you were born neither the obstetrician nor the midwife noticed that your feet were different. I noticed immediately, as soon as I saw you. I was cradling you in my arms while the obstetrician cut the umbilical cord and I remember clearly telling him that there was something different about your feet. I never said there was something wrong, or abnormal, I clearly remember using the word different. We opened the blanket that you were swaddled in and one of your feet was very narrow, too narrow.

My initial thoughts in those long minutes after your birth are exactly the same as my thoughts today. When something happens, something that differs from your expectation of a situation or an event — I am loath to say something normal or something abnormal as I do not think these are constructive expressions — it is important that you remember that there is always an upside, identify the positive aspects and then concentrate on them.

As you grew, we spent our time going from one specialist to the next, in all we saw eleven doctors. And you forget, there was no internet back then to use as a research tool. We would hear of a doctor in America by word of mouth and then attempt to fax or telephone him, but it was never straightforward as often the numbers were incorrect and then of course the doctors were busy so they did not necessarily get back to us immediately. We were often caught between faxing for a second time at the risk of harassing the doctor or waiting and dealing with our own anxiety and stress levels. When it is your child, you need to get to the bottom of the situation as soon as possible, find out as much as you can, work out what the best options are and what decisions you have to take.

In the end we narrowed down the list to three experts and then engineered a time and a place convenient to all of them so that they could meet up and finally discuss your situation face to face. I am sure each doctor remembers that meeting to this day. As you know, one of the three was Gerry Versveld. Their conclusions were as follows: amputation of your right leg was absolutely necessary as you were missing the necessary bones, the situation for your left leg was more complex and it was probable that reconstructive surgery would be successful. Gerry then told me about a biannual medical convention focusing purely on the science behind bilateral amputations that was about to take place. I phoned the convention organisers and explained to them that I wanted to send our specialist, Gerry Versveld (he was very well known and had previously been invited to that same convention), with all of the relevant photographic and X-ray documentation regarding my son's condition so that his case could be examined by the convention. Fortunately for all of us, they agreed and so it was that Gerry came and delivered his paper on your condition before over three hundred of the world's top specialists and solicited their input. The consensus was unanimous: they recommended a bilateral amputation below the knee. Although it was never easy for us, we were relieved as we felt we had done everything possible to receive the best advice.

Of course, the hardest part was still to come.

Gerry advised us to amputate as soon as possible, but crucially before you learnt to walk. He explained to us that if you never learnt to walk on your own feet you would never experience the trauma of no longer having feet to walk on and so you would also learn to walk with the prosthetic limbs with ease. Gerry explained to us that he would amputate at the ankle joint and then transplant the skin from your heels onto the end of your stumps so as to make them stronger and more resistant and capable of bearing your body weight as well as the friction that would occur with future prostheses. We had pressed Gerry to explain the operation in detail to us, but let me tell you my boy, it did not make for easy listening. The reality of the operation was terrible for us. As a baby your feet were so delicate and ticklish, we spent a lot of time with you lying next to us as we cuddled you and tickled your feet while you giggled adorably. The thought of the doctors cutting off your feet and throwing them in the rubbish bin was almost too much to bear. Something I would not even wish on my worst enemy.

Thank God, the operation went well and your recovery was exceptional. Your first prosthetic limbs were without moulded feet on the end: you looked like a little pirate with them on and once you got the hang of it there was no holding you back, you were incapable of sitting still, and the house echoed with the clippety clap tapping noise that your prostheses made as you raced around.

You were a confident, strong and happy child. Sheila — like any other mother — instinctively tried to help you and be there for you whenever you found yourself in difficulty. I tried to discourage this because I felt that by helping you she would be doing you more harm than good. I was much harder on you (sometimes even cruel) because I knew that you needed to be self-sufficient always. I was more exacting of you than I have been with Carl but it was because I knew that you would encounter more obstacles in your life: children are not always nice to one another and far more often than we like to admit bully those that are different from them. That is just how life is and I wanted to make sure that if you were ever in difficulty and I was not there to help you, you would be capable of sorting it out for yourself.

When you were small, I made a point of not interfering, I just watched over you from the sidelines. You always knew that at home you would be able to discuss whatever had taken place. Often we talked about people's reactions to you and explained that they did not understand, that they were ignorant and that it was your responsibility to explain things to them. I think these experiences are at the heart of you being such a good communicator and a people person.

Your mother became pregnant again not long after your operation and I remember you and Carl buzzing around her like two little bees always eager to put your hands on her stomach to feel the baby move.

Then when Aimée was born, I will never forget your amazement as you said: 'Look, she has feet!' We never paid much attention to your behaviour but whenever you could, once your mother had placed Aimée back in her cradle, fast asleep, you would come along, greet her with the nickname you invented for her, Gugu, and then remove her blanket and kiss her little feet. You drove your mother nuts as you inevitably woke Aimée and then she had to start the laborious process of getting her back to sleep all over again. You have always been a spontaneous person, as soon as you feel something in your heart you act on it and there is a lot that is endearing in your behaviour. We knew also that your curiosity was natural and so we left you to your discovery. We often discussed your behaviour; we called it the 'Oscar Pistorius Model'. You were meant to be just as you were and are and we were determined to accept you without trying to hide you or change you and I think this made all the difference for each of us.

There were support groups for children and parents who had also experienced similar amputations but quickly Sheila and I realised that although we would be able to help many of the parents present, few if any there were going to be of help to us. The issue is all about attitude and most often it is the parent's attitude to the child, and not the child him or herself, that causes problems.

I remember one particular meeting of the support group in Johannesburg. A woman with her daughter was walking just in front of me. The daughter was a beautiful blonde child with a lovely smile but without any arms. I knew of course that we were headed towards the same meeting, when suddenly the woman told her child to come this way as on that side there were too many people that were sure to stare at her. I was horrified: how can a mother say such a thing to her child? It is the mother who is the problem, not the child. I was profoundly upset by what I heard and so when the meeting began I stood up and told everyone present that this was my last meeting because I was convinced that the majority of the adults in the room, there supposedly to learn and give support to amputees, were actually part of the problem. It was their attitudes that created such difficulty in the lives of their children.

Thank God you have never had this problem. You have always been at ease with yourself and proud of who you are. Everything has come naturally to you. Even when you first wore your prosthetic limbs, they were brand new but within a day they looked like you had had them for months. They were scratched and chipped because you were always running around, climbing and colliding with objects, you were fearless, then you would come back to me with that mischievous smile of yours and say, 'Look, Dad, I have a bruise!'

Your smile is unchanged, my dear son, as is your strength of character and happy-go-lucky approach to life. My wish for your future is that your smile remains as light and pure as it is today and that you continue to see new challenges after each marvellous achievement.

Your Dad

We do hope that you have enjoyed reading
this large print book.

Did you know that all of our titles
are available for purchase?

We publish a wide range of high quality
large print books including:
Romances, Mysteries, Classics
General Fiction
Non Fiction and Westerns

Special interest titles available in
large print are:
The Little Oxford Dictionary
Music Book
Song Book
Hymn Book
Service Book

Also available from us courtesy of Oxford
University Press:
Young Readers' Dictionary
(large print edition)
Young Readers' Thesaurus
(large print edition)

For further information or a free
brochure, please contact us at:
Ulverscroft Large Print Books Ltd.,
The Green, Bradgate Road, Anstey,
Leicester, LE7 7FU, England.
Tel: (00 44) 0116 236 4325
Fax: (00 44) 0116 234 0205